Ethics and the Beast

A SPECIESIST ARGUMENT FOR ANIMAL LIBERATION

Tzachi Zamir

PRINCETON UNIVERSITY PRESS

PRINCETON AND OXFORD

Copyright © 2007 by Princeton University Press

Published by Princeton University Press, 41 William Street,
Princeton, New Jersey 08540

In the United Kingdom: Princeton University Press, 3 Market Place,
Woodstock, Oxfordshire OX20 1SY

Library of Congress Cataloging-in-Publication Data

Zamir, Tzachi, 1967–

Ethics and the beast : a speciesist argument for animal liberation / Tzachi Zamir.
p. cm.

ISBN-13: 978-0-691-13328-7 ((hardcover) : alk. paper)
1. Animal welfare—Moral and ethical aspects.   2. Speciesism.   I. Title.
HV4708.Z36 2007
179′.3—dc22
2007007155

British Library Cataloging-in-Publication Data is available
This book has been composed in Sabon

Printed on acid-free paper. ∞

press.princeton.edu

Printed in the United States of America

1   3   5   7   9   10   8   6   4   2

Dedicated to Iddo Landau and Daniel Statman

———————————

CONTENTS

ACKNOWLEDGMENTS

THIS BOOK BEGAN from a series of arguments over several lunches with Richard Posner of the University of Chicago, who challenged me to defend my moral vegetarianism. I did not fair well, and so I began to sketch an argument that eventually developed into this book. I thank him for prompting me to take up animal ethics seriously.

For comments on individual chapters, I am indebted to Shuli Barzilai, Stan Godlovitch, Nathan Nobis, Tom Regan, Nahum Shpiegel, Alon Wasserman, and Eddy Zemach. Godlovitch and Zemach have significantly influenced and challenged my thoughts at several important stages, and I am grateful to both for discussing drafts with me. I am also obliged to Horst Spielmann, head of ZEBET, for a generous invitation to the 5th World Congress on Alternatives and Animal Use in the Life Sciences (Berlin, 2005). Some of the alternative-related information presented in the fourth chapter was obtained in that conference.

Substantial comments on the manuscript as a whole were provided by the three reviewers of the book. I would like to thank Peter Singer and the two anonymous reviewers for the wise, constructive, and generous comments that they made.

I cannot assess the degree to which my thoughts on animals have been influenced by my wife, Orit. I feel sure that her being a veterinarian, more than enabling me to repeatedly verify points of fact when writing this, has enveloped me for many years in the concerns and moral dilemmas that hands-on work with animals involves. Her moral vegetarianism preceded mine, and I am certain that her example has led to my own decisions. I am grateful for both her help and her influence.

Iddo Landau and Daniel Statman have both provided valuable comments on chapters in this book. But they have also enabled it in a very real sense by courageously supporting me in complex circumstances. Their inspiring attitude exemplifies, for me, moral integrity under pressure. I dedicate this book to them.

Some of the chapters have been published in earlier forms as journal articles. Chapter 1 was published in *Philosophia*. Chapters 2 and 3 were published in *Between the Species*; chapter 4 in the *Journal of Applied Philosophy*; chapter 6 in the *Journal of Social Philosophy*; and chapters 7 and 8 in *Society and Animals*. I thank these journals for permission to modify and incorporate this material here.

INTRODUCTION

"Speciesist-liberationism" seems a contradiction in terms. Yet this book offers an elaboration of precisely this position, presenting it as the one that liberationists and nonliberationists should endorse. Calling this a "defense" of speciesist liberationism would somewhat misrepresent the book's argument, since I avoid showing why speciesism is itself justified. My concern is, rather, to show how a detailed case for reforming our attitude toward nonhuman animals need not involve abandoning widely shared speciesist intuitions.[1] Deradicalization of the theoretical underpinnings of liberationism is important not merely because it is philosophically correct, or because it trims the debate over animal ethics of surplus detailed arguments. The more significant benefit of a theoretical minimization of the case for reform is tapping a broader consensus. Weighty practical ramifications follow from conservative, widely shared, moral beliefs.

The book's first two chapters rework the more abstract considerations underlying liberationism. I begin by showing that speciesism contradicts liberationism only under an overly strong and unintuitive rendering of the term. After claiming that liberationism is continuous with virtually all of our speciesist intuitions, the next chapter pinpoints another unfortunate detour that currently burdens reform: the case for the "moral status" of animals. The chapter aims to rid liberationism of the need to establish such "status." After rewriting the case for reform, the book proceeds to detailed examination of particular practices in which animals are either killed or used. The third chapter presents a defense of moral vegetarianism that does not rely on the vegetarian's capacity to influence large-scale outcome. My argument against animal-based experiments (chapter 4) utilizes the speciesist-liberationist position by showing that the speciesist assumptions that typically justify research can themselves be accepted, yet doing so is consistent with a rejection of vivisection.

---

[1] Throughout this book the terms "animal" and "nonhuman animal" will refer to all nonhuman animals that humans have (companion animals, zoo and circus animals), use (farm animals), or kill (for food, scientific knowledge, product safety, and hunting). I will not distinguish between high and low animals (so my discussion covers practices relating to fish and crabs). I will say little about insects, not because they are not animals, but because they are relevant only to the morality of "pest" control, a discussion that in my opinion we are presently ill-equipped to develop. Anatomically, the terms animal and nonhuman animal will cover entities possessing nervous systems, rudimentary as well as complex systems, that may indicate the existence of pain or suffering.

The book's final part, on using animals, formulates and defends a distinction between exploitation and use (chapter 5). The use/exploitation distinction then mobilizes a response to two questions that have received scant attention in the past. The first is whether liberationists should be moral vegetarians or moral vegans. Chapter 6 examines the moral viability of using "farm animals" even if they are not killed for their flesh. The next question is whether employing animals as therapeutic means is morally blameless from a liberationist perspective (chapter 7). The book closes with a rejection of the welfare-based defense of zoos.

Throughout the book, the reader will note a repeated concern to finesse thorny issues and to focus only on what is absolutely essential for the liberationist's moral argument. Apart from decluttering the case for reform, a second notable overarching motif of the book is addressing issues that have been left programmatic or vague in the first and second waves of books on animal ethics. Liberationists are often challenged to specify the precise scope of their proposals. Yet understandably enough, the best philosophical work on animals from the 1970s on had to focus on creating a larger gestalt shift than entering issues that are themselves internally debated within animal movements. It is time to broach these issues, and to spell out further what liberationism means. A third common thread woven into the following discussions is the surprising flexibility that liberationism prescribes in contrast to the all/nothing expectation that is often associated with animal ethics.

The book strives to respect nonphilosophers who may be interested in individual topics but are unversed in the technical jargon of moral philosophy. The first two chapters do assume some familiarity with previous contributions to animal ethics and are perhaps not a suitable introduction. Yet they facilitate reading by an informed nonphilosopher, who may wonder about the viability of speciesist-liberationism given the conventional coordinates of the debate. I have tried to preserve some overlap between the chapters to enable reading a discussion of a specific subject without digesting the argument of the book as a whole.

PART I

Ethics and Beasts

Chapter 1

IS SPECIESISM OPPOSED TO LIBERATIONISM?

EVER SINCE RYDER AND SINGER introduced the term, "speciesism" has been seen as the arch opponent of those who strive to reform our relations with animals. While much is achieved by compelling people to critically evaluate their species-related biases, my contention in this book is that allowing the speciesist/nonspeciesist opposition to govern the call to rethink the moral status of animals is significantly misleading, unnecessary, and detrimental to this important cause. Throughout this chapter I will attempt to distill a sense of "speciesism" that actually opposes the pro-animal claim. It will be shown that endorsing the more intuitive meanings of speciesism should not trouble liberationists. Consequently, there is no need to replace speciesist intuitions in order to support reform. Speciesism becomes a target for reformers only under an overly strong and unintuitive sense.

"SPECIESISM" AND "LIBERATIONISM"

I need to begin by clarifying what the terms speciesism and liberationism mean throughout this book. "Speciesism" has not been used in a uniform sense in the literature. The term goes back to the beginnings of liberationist literature in the 1970s. R. D. Ryder gives the following characterization: "Speciesism and racism are both forms of prejudice that are based upon appearances—if the other individual looks different then he is rated as being beyond the moral pale. Racism is today condemned by most intelligent and compassionate people and it seems only logical that such people should extend their concern for other races to other species also."[1] Peter Singer's introduction of the concept also appeals to prejudice: "Speciesism—the word is not an attractive one, but I can think of no better term—is a prejudice of attitude of bias toward the interests of members of one's own species and against those of members of other species."[2] David DeGrazia too perceives the notion as referring

---

[1] R. D. Ryder, *Victims of Science: The Use of Animals in Research* (London: National Anti-Vivisection Society Limited, 1983 [1975]), 5.
[2] Peter Singer, *Animal Liberation* (New York: Avon Books, 1975), 7.

to "unjustified discrimination against animals."[3] Tom Regan uses the term less to describe prejudice, and more as a way of dissociating animals from moral entitlement: "A speciesist position, at least the paradigm of such a position, would take the form of declaring that no animal is a member of the moral community because no animal belongs to the "right" species—namely, *Homo sapiens*."[4] Mark Bernstein's characterization of the term ties species membership with morally relevant properties, which, in turn, legitimates discounting interests of nonmembers: "Speciesists believe that membership in a particular species is morally relevant. Morally relevant properties entitle their possessors to have their interests considered preferentially relative to those individuals who lack that property."[5] These senses overlap but are not equivalent, and throughout this chapter I will attempt to distill a precise sense of the term that contradicts liberationism.

As for "liberationism" (reaching back to Singer's *Animal Liberation*, a book that has revived the modern version of animal ethics), I shall use "liberationists" and "liberationism" as umbrella terms covering many distinct views that have in common:

A. The belief that nonhuman animals are systematically expelled from the pale of substantial moral consideration either by objectification or by downplaying the manner by which moral concerns ought to inform our animal-related conduct.
B. The sense that numerous animal-related practices ought to be substantially reformed or eliminated.
C. An undertaking of a transformation in one's own personal conduct in relation to animal-related practices. For example, boycotting some commodities, or modifying one's diet, clothing, footwear, or choice of cosmetics (all or some of these are sufficient for C).

To be less abstract, the term "liberationists" includes philosophers such as Singer, Regan, Godlovitch, Ryder, DeGrazia, Sapontzis, and Cavalieri as well as other philosophers who write on behalf of animals and are less widely known. I am thinking, too, of numerous nonphilosophers who are advocating a general and substantial reform in our conduct to animals.

---

[3] David DeGrazia, *Taking Animals Seriously: Mental Life and Moral Status* (New York: Cambridge University Press, 1996), 28.

[4] Tom Regan, *The Case for Animals Rights* (Berkeley: University of California Press, 1985), 155.

[5] Mark Bernstein, "Neo-Speciesism," *Journal of Social Philosophy* 35 (3) (2004): 380. For a more general discussion including variations of speciesism, see P. Cavalieri, *The Animal Question: Why Nonhuman Animals Deserve Human Rights*, trans. C. Woollard (New York: Oxford University Press, 2001), chap. 4.

SPECIESISM

Speciesism is sometimes identified with believing that membership in the human species is a morally relevant property. Liberationists have no cause to object to this sense because it is not exclusive: a speciesist of this kind can *also* believe that being a nonhuman animal is a morally relevant property as well. Such a speciesist can even be an active liberationist. Should liberationists oppose a formulation of speciesism according to which humanity is the *only* species in which membership constitutes a morally relevant property? They should not. This formulation too can be digested by a liberationist, who can accept humanity as some special category, distinct from all other species, yet also hold that moral considerability should extend to any being who possesses a capacity for negative experience. This would mean that, unlike humans, it is not by virtue of species membership that animals should not be treated in certain ways, but due to their capacity to suffer or be deprived of valuable experiences. The mere identification of species membership as a morally relevant property should not bother liberationists.

Similarly, a mere assertion of human superiority should not, on its own, bother liberationists. Say that someone holds the following (highly popular) position:

Speciesism (1): Humans are more important than nonhumans because they are human.

Let us ignore possible justifications for this position and focus on what it entails. Liberationists can wholeheartedly agree to (1), yet refuse to see why or how this self-commending assertion is connected to any discounting of animal interests. In fact, forging a link between this definition and overriding interests is possible, but not immediate. The greater value of humans is sometimes taken to be *identical* with claiming that human interests override the interests of nonhuman animals, as if they mean one and the same. But this identification is mistaken. There exists no simple semantic equivalence between greater value and trumping interests. Some of the things we value have no interests at all (e.g., works of art). Of the things that do have interests, it is possible and plausible to sometimes allow the interests of the less valued entity to overmaster the interests of the more valuable one. One can, for example, agree that the value of the lives of numerous strangers living in some distant country outweighs the value of the life of one's child, yet still allow the interests of the latter to take priority. A factory may value Bill more than other workers yet refuse to discount the interests of other workers when they clash with Bill's.

"Greater value" (leaving the nature of this open) does not simply *mean* discounting interests. But perhaps weaker connections than semantic equivalence are able to tie value to trumping interests. Does the greater value of A over B *entail* the devaluing of B's interests when these conflict with B's? Or, short of logical necessity, does greater importance make such favoritism *plausible*? If the above counterexamples to semantic equivalence make sense, then the answer is negative here too. Susan will save her aging father before she rescues an important scientist even if she admits that the latter's life is more valuable. Greater value (even if it can be conclusively determined) is only one of several considerations that jointly determine whose interests come first. Consider, too, the opposite direction: preferential policies hardly ever appeal to importance, and they can easily belittle the importance of importance. Countries, for example, are obliged to help their own citizens before they assist others. Yet this preferential policy does not stem from a belief in the greater value of these citizens, and it may even be endorsed by a government that, for some bizarre reason, believes that its own citizens are less important. The assumptions that appear relevant here relate to what being a citizen means and the special obligations that this imposes. In sum: greater importance does not hook (logically or probably) onto a discounting of interests.

A critic can object to these counterexamples. "Ideally," the critic may argue, "Susan should save the scientist rather than her father, and parents ought to discount the interests of their children if they substantially compromise the well-being of numerous strangers." The critic will go on to say that the inability to comply with moral demands in the tough cases above merely indicates that we are willing to forgive some discrepancies between morally ideal and actual conduct. Excusing such behavior should not be confused with annulling the connection between superiority and trumping interests: the interests of the important scientist or those distant valuable strangers should still morally precede the interests of less valuable entities. "Moral saints"—the Agamemnons of this world who are willing to sacrifice their Iphigenias in order to save their armies—would act accordingly.

This criticism should be rejected. To begin with, the criticism rests on a crude utilitarianism that would be dismissed not only by nonutilitarians, but also by contemporary, nuanced utilitarian positions. Contemporary utilitarians strive to respect a detailed and complex interplay between maximizing value and responding to particular attachments, trying to accommodate these attachments as part of what "maximizing value" should mean.[6] The assiduous efforts on the part of utilitarians to show that they are not necessarily committed to forsaking their kin or friends on behalf of some important stranger in themselves register the desire to maintain utilitarian decision making free from some automatic linkage

---

[6] For one such discussion on the role of special obligations, see R. M. Hare, *Moral Thinking: Its Levels, Method and Point* (Oxford: Oxford University Press, 1981), chap. 8.

between import and discounting interests. Nonutilitarians, on the other hand, would find such reasoning to be not merely counterintuitive, but also oblivious to our moral commitments to family members. It is morally desirable that people save their relatives rather than act according to import. The ties between obligations to family and one's conduct are stronger (and ought to be so when preventing impending harm) than the link between relative importance and conduct. Saying that we are "morally excused" when acting in accordance with such commitments, that ideal or supererogatory conduct does call for such sacrifice, is implicated in a theoretical insensitivity to these particular obligations. Moreover, even if the critic is right about ideal morality, s/he is (ultimately) wrong in terms of the criticism's objective in our context. Significantly, the capacity to seriously question whether or not ideal morality prescribes sacrifices in "Iphigenia cases" registers indecisive links between import and discounting interests. Accordingly, the connection between superiority and trumping interests is not immediate on the level of either moral conduct or ideal moral conduct.

The critic can now reformulate the objection: the examples above merely show that the connection between superior value and trumping interests is defeasible through the workings of special overpowering considerations—not that it is not there at all. Some considerations (familial attachment, national solidarity or loyalty) can annul the linkage between superiority and trumping interests, a connection that is there all the same. Put another way, the examples prove that we are willing to refrain from advancing the interests of entities that we value more when these clash with very strong attachments and commitments we have to particular people. In the case of nonhuman animals, however, such attachments are beside the point. We not only disvalue them relative to humans, but we have no real reason to abandon our predilection to favor interests of the more valuable entities, namely, ourselves. Our conclusion should have been that, all things being (in some undefined sense) equal, if A is superior to B, A's interests should be preferred. In the context of defining speciesism, we thus reach the following:

Speciesism (2): Humans are more important than nonhumans because they are humans, and therefore, all things being equal, their interests should be preferred.

Let us avoid harping on the vagueness of "importance" and "all things being equal" or pressurizing the "because they are human" clause (this last construction being a favorite target of liberationists). Considerations going back at least to Plato's *Gorgias* will show that this definition, even if the central operators in it can be unpacked in a credible way, is still insufficient in generating antiliberationism.

Suppose that I am having A and B to dinner, and that all of us, including B, recognize A's superiority over B and myself (say that A has just received a Nobel Prize, and that B and myself wholeheartedly believe that this constitutes a reason to regard him as categorically superior in value to us). Moreover, we all agree that this means that "all things being equal," A's interests ought to take priority over our own. The vagueness in (2) relates to the inability to stipulate credible links between such beliefs and *particular* decisions regarding specific clashes of interests. For example, should A receive larger portions of food because of his relative importance? Should he have the last slice of pie, which all of us have been coveting, due to his seniority? Should he be the one that gets to determine the temperature level of the air conditioning system? The sense of ridicule stems not only from our inability to seriously fathom the idea that one human being is superior to another, but from the intrinsic improbability of meticulously tying greater value and consequent belief in trumping interests with *specific* entitlements. Even if all three of us agree both that A is superior and that this should entail *some* kind of promotion of his interests over our own, this admission does not tie up neatly to favoritism of a *particular* kind.

Noting the lacuna between some general favoritism and particular entitlements is important. Liberationists can endorse the second version of speciesism above, accepting both the idea that humans are more important as well as the idea that human interests come first, yet, because this definition does not determine *which* animal interests should be disfavored, add that accepting such beliefs still coheres with abolishment of virtually all animal-related exploitative practices (the definition obviously does not commit one to saying that *any* human interest overrides any nonhuman one). Accepting the second definition of speciesism does not, for example, entail that particular human culinary interests justify killing animals in order to satisfy those interests. Nor does it support the notion that human research interests exonerate killing and confining millions of rodents (I shall discuss life vs. life conflicts below). Moreover, "trumping" or "coming first" are importantly vague.

TRUMPING INTERESTS

Brody has profitably distinguished between two forms of the "trumping human interest" claim.[7] The first is categorical: any human interest,

---

[7] B. A. Brody, "Defending Animal Research: An International Perspective," in *Why Animal Experimentation Matters: The Use of Animals in Medical Research*, ed. E. F. Paul and J. Paul, 131–48 (New Brunswick: Transaction Publishers, 2001).

regardless of importance, overrides any animal interest (Brody calls this "lexical priority"). The second is weaker: some human interests carry more weight than some animal interests (Brody calls this "discounting of interests"). Important animal interests (their interest to live or avoid pain) should trump minor human interests. Brody uses this distinction in his mapping of policies for restricting animal-based experiments (associating U.S. policies with lexical priority; European ones with discounting). I add that the categorical (lexical priority) version can be broken down further into qualitative and quantitative aspects: for advocates of the qualitative categorical position, any human interest overrides any nonhuman interest, regardless of the relative importance of the particular interests involved. For defenders of the quantitative categorical variant, any human interest overrides the interest of any nonhuman entity, regardless of the *number* of beings whose interests are affected.

An additional relevant distinction here relates to unpacking "trumping," into a distinction between the obligation to help and the permission to hurt.[8] Say that I believe that A's interests take priority over B's in the sense that they are overriding when in conflict. This can mean that I am obligated to help A or to promote any of A's interests before I assist B (if I see myself as obliged to assist B at all). This is far from supposing that I am entitled to hurt B or curtail any of B's interests so as to benefit A. This distinction is routinely recognized in human contexts: my commitment to assist my child does not extend to a vindication of me actively harming other children in order to advance my own. While aiding my child can be detrimental to other children, as long as I did nothing actively and directly against them, there is nothing immoral in my actions.

A speciesist holding on to this version regarding what "trumping" means can still be a liberationist: she will see herself as obliged to assist humans and to promote their interests before she helps animals. She can even endorse a categorical version of the trumping claim (both qualitatively and quantitatively), believing that it is her duty to promote marginal human interests before she advances cardinal nonhuman ones, even ones that affect only a small number of human beings (e.g., she can volunteer to give music appreciation classes in a poor neighborhood rather than tend to sick loose animals). But she will *not* believe that this permits her to actively suppress an animal's interest so as to advance a human one. And she will thus be a fully committed liberationist, demanding that all animal-related exploitative practices should immediately cease.

Even speciesism that holds to a categorical version of trumping interests in Brody's sense is, then, continuous with a robust liberationist agenda. In nontechnical terms: one can believe that human beings are

---

[8] M. Bernstein calls these type A and type B actions. "Neo-Speciesism," 380–91.

more important than animals, that their interests come first in the sense that any human interest takes precedence over that of a nonhuman animal (meaning that it is morally obligatory to advance any human interest before advancing any animal interest), yet still not only refuse to actively thwart animal interests, but also be an abolitionist regarding most animal-related practices.

It now appears that the form of speciesism that actually opposes liberationism is this:

> Speciesism (3): It is justified to *actively* thwart the interests of a nonhuman animal when they conflict with the interests of a human animal, and it is justified to do so because these are human interests.

But (3) still fails to constitute antiliberationism because it lacks restrictions specifying the relative importance of the conflicting interests. Even stout liberationists would not be troubled over minor discounting of animal interests (ships crossing the ocean may alarm fish as they pass, yet I know of no activist who would oppose naval travel on this basis). To generate antiliberationism, the overridden interests of the animal must be substantial while the human interests are marginal.

Here we enter a more substantive dimension of the debate. If liberationists admit that minor nonhuman interests may be discounted, they might get pushed to admit that substantial human interests justify actively discounting nonhuman interests. Liberationists would oppose this contention (rightly in my opinion). But at this point the debate usually degenerates into survival, lifeboat scenarios. These involve challenging liberationists through conjuring situations involving human/nonhuman life/death conflicts (saving a man through tossing a dog overboard when only one can be saved implies a speciesist bias, and so the liberationist is supposed to be embarrassed into admitting her own tacit speciesism). There are various liberationist counterarguments to this.[9] Yet I do not think that liberationists need to worry about such contrived cases. They can bite the bullet, admitting that in life/death situations they would promote human survival even if this meant actively killing an animal. Yet they would add that allowing survival to be a trumping interest does not imply that other highly important human interests are also trumping. Liberationists could thus endorse speciesism of the following kind:

> Speciesism (4): It is justified to *actively* thwart the survival interests of a nonhuman being when they conflict with survival interests of a

[9] These are usually arguments by analogy, claiming that the same reasoning cannot be applied in human-human lifeboat cases. The problem with these analogies is that in an antispeciesist context, they beg the question in assuming that intuitions generated from interhuman moral transactions carry over smoothly to human-animal ones.

human animal, and it is justified to do so because these are human interests.

When endorsing (4), liberationists will add that the numerous exploitative animal-related practices that they are criticizing do not resemble lifeboat situations in the least. The varied forms of animal abuse (factory-farms, most animal-based research, zoos, blood sports, fishing or hunting) should be abolished, even if one admits that in survival scenarios one would be a fierce speciesist.

The only animal-related practice that does perhaps resemble the lifeboat scenario is experimentation on animals as part of applied research in which life-saving drugs are developed and tested. While liberationists argue against imaging research in terms of a lifeboat situation (both in terms of the disanalogies that this picture obfuscates and also in terms of the moral logic itself[10]), there is one way in which digesting the speciesist intuitions that emerge from imaginary lifeboats actually advances the liberationist cause. As I argue further on in this book in a detailed chapter devoted to experimentation (chapter 4), most research consists of product testing, classroom demonstrations, and basic research (which is many times unconnected to any known human illness). This means that *if* liberationists and scientists agree that animal-dependent research ought to continue wherever human survival is at stake (while at the same time relocating funds for the purpose of developing alternatives to such research models, thereby eliminating the "lifeboat" nature of research, even if it is such[11]), most animal-related research will have to stop. This result is not ideal. Yet it serves the liberationist agenda and will be an extremely important step forward for liberationism. Promoting a tough and radical liberationist agenda is thus continuous with speciesism as defined in this fourth definition when "trumping" is confined to survival conflicts.

Before moving on to a modified version of the fourth definition, which does finally constitute an antiliberationist position, I need to respond to a liberationist worry about slippery slopes having to do with the linkage between survival interests and other important interests. The liberationist counterargument to what I have just conceded on behalf of liberationists is that if one allows survival interests to take precedence, one appears to admit that important human interests justify actively annulling interests

---

[10] See Bernstein, "Neo-Speciesism"; S. Finsen, "Sinking the Research Lifeboat," *Journal of Medicine and Philosophy* 13 (1988): 197–212; and D. Jamieson and T. Regan, "On the Ethics of the Use of Animals in Science," in *Ethical Issues in Scientific Research*, ed. E. Erwin, S. Gendin, and L. Kleiman, 267–302 (New York: Garland, 1994).

[11] Is fund-allocation itself in such cases a lifeboat of a kind (since one is, in effect, devoting resources to the well-being of animals when such funding could have been channeled to studies that might prevent diseases that endanger humans)? This may have made sense if all research funds were devoted to human survival.

of animals. But if liberationists concede this, they would be pressed to make further concessions. After all, why limit importance to survival? What about great human suffering induced by minor aesthetic flaws that can be eliminated through animal-based devising of cosmetics? Basic research (the interest to know) or fine cuisine (the interest to enjoy higher pleasure and a richer life) will find defenders maintaining that these are important human interests. Liberationists would worry that accepting the fourth definition above is not limited merely to swallowing the speciesist intuitions in lifeboat situations, but extends to legitimating all kinds of animal-exploitative practices that promote important human interests, and that *pace* the pacifying tone of my argument, this last implication *is* detrimental to liberationism. There is thus a slippery slope leading from survival to other human interests. Justifying the first would vindicate the others too.

Yet like other philosophically credible responses to slippery slopes, a liberationist can draw the line very high: human survival trumps animal survival, yet nothing short of survival does. Drawing the line in this way is consistent since making anti-animal concessions in survival conflicts does not carry over logically or probably to other concessions. Interhuman survival conflicts, for example, also modify our moral intuitions: we justify extreme conduct in such situations that we will not extend to scenarios that do not involve survival. Secondly, slippery slopes work both ways: if an antiliberationist places too much importance on slippery slopes, and if she admits that some marginal human interests should not override highly important animal ones, for example, admitting that some experiments should not be done, or that maltreating animals is possible, then the slippery slope would work its way up: if animals are not to be tortured, what legitimates locking them up in zoos? If their interests count for something, what prevents them from counting for more?

We can now formulate the active discounting speciesist definition that does finally oppose liberationism, since it includes quantitative and qualitative determination:

> Speciesism (5): Non-survival-related human interests, important as well as marginal ones, legitimately trump major interests of nonhumans (in the sense that it is justified to actively disadvantage nonhuman animals, even when such privileging significantly affects a large number of them). Such privileging is justified because these trumping interests belong to humans.

It is this version of speciesism that legitimizes any of the actual animal-related exploitative practices that liberationists would like to abolish, and it is the only one that they need to argue against. Speciesism in any of the previous senses should not trouble liberationists.

Justifying Speciesism

I have so far claimed that many versions of speciesism are consistent with liberationism. But I have not yet said why speciesism is itself justified. This aspect of my argument is less important because I am less worried about the viability of speciesism as such and more concerned about correcting some distortions in the present debates over animals. "If speciesism is false, liberationism scores points or is even mandatory." Such, I think, is the underlying motivation of much pro-animal writing when it addresses speciesism. The argument proposed here is different: attempting to deconstruct speciesist intuitions is beside the moral point. Robust liberationism is conceptually and practically continuous with these traditional intuitions (even if they are false).

Still, is there any reason why we should retain our speciesist biases? The problem with rigorously justifying speciesism surfaces when one attempts to unpack the greater importance of humans over nonhumans. Judgments over relative importance presuppose a frame of reference that, in the case of animal ethics, begs the question: properties that human beings value induce us to fallaciously accept an overall value judgment concerning a species as such. The fallacy stems from our agnosticism regarding animal minds. We cannot assess what animals value for the obvious reason that they do not appear to make value judgments. The most meaningful thing we say is that we care more for humans, and that humans are more important to us. This, obviously, does not justify the belief that humans are generally more important, unless one assumes that the general and the human are one and the same. Once again, this would beg the question against animals.

Let us generalize the issue. Can we ever justify a sense in which X is more important than Y? Subjective importance makes sense of such judgments ("X is more valuable *to me* than Y"). But such subjective usage is useless when defending speciesism: if all we are able to say is that humans value other humans over animals, we cannot infer that humans are in fact more valuable than animals. Crack addicts value a drug more than food. Yet this need not imply that drugs are more important than food. This holds unless the human frame of reference is taken to be all-important, an assumption that would beg the question against animals and what might be important to them. Literature that supports speciesism offers three answers to this apparent impasse: first, assertions of human superiority based on some greater potential or by alluding to special properties that humans possess, properties that make humans more important; second, upholding species solidarity (which thus grounds particular obligations to members of one's own species over

other beings); third, reclaiming some of the more traditional anchors of
speciesism (humans have a soul; animals do not, or humans have divine
permission to regard themselves as superior to other animals). Liberationists have offered strong arguments against each of these, and I do not
intend to rehash this debate here.

Yet does my inclination to throw a dog overboard in order to save a
drowning woman actually stem from a sense of solidarity, or from the
greater potential of her life in contrast to the dog's? Does tossing the dog
emerge from my grasp of a particular obligation I have to the woman?
Am I moved to act because of my awareness that she has a soul/can rea-
son/can communicate in an elaborate manner? I think not. Something
more basic appears to be going on when such decisions take place. One
is tempted to use the word "instinct" here, as such decisions appear to
resemble instinctive actions, such as fighting to save one's child, at whatever cost to others. One is not acting from a sense of moral duty or obligation. These concepts can be used after the fact to justify in hindsight an
action that issued out of more immediate and less cerebral routes. It
might be true that most human lives are richer than the lives of animals.
Some of us may also experience an overwhelming sense of solidarity with
other humans. Others might think that humans have rights that animals
do not possess, and therefore one should attach more weight to their interests. But such claims, even if admitted, appear to be less of a reason
for action, and more of an attempt to justify a strongly held intuition.

Moral philosophers (rightly) regard intuitions gingerly. But since this is
not the place to plunge into the debate over intuitions, their value (or lack
thereof), and whether or not moral reasoning can be purged of them, I will
appeal to a conservative theoretical principle: choose your battles when
advocating reform—avoid replacing existing beliefs/intuitions/considered
judgments that can be harmlessly maintained. Rescuing the woman by
pitching the dog overboard does not appear to me to conflict with or con-
tradict my own liberationist sensitivities. It does cohere with my speciesist
bias to promote the welfare of humans before that of animals, even if the
humans happen to be profoundly retarded and inferior in mental capacities in relation to the animals. And it constitutes precisely the kind of case
in which I am prompted to actively discount the interests of an animal.
The same holds for eating animals: if personal or collective survival requires eating animal flesh, I would give up my moral vegetarianism. The
justification I can give to this does not amount to anything more sophisti-
cated than an engrained favoritism. Similar deep-seated intuitions underlie
my liberationism: primarily, the immediate, nonderived conviction that
needless tremendous suffering and death take place, and that these can
and should be eradicated.

Lifeboat situations thus do elicit a speciesist intuition in me, which I see no reason to shun. Yet a second moral intuition that surfaces in me when considering lifeboat cases and that I should record is the inclination to look for ways by which survival conflict can be dissolved and through which lifeboat "either/or" decisions can be finessed. The only lifeboat-like situation with regard to interspecies ethics relates (perhaps) to a very small portion of applied research. Allocating substantial resources to alternative research models might make this conflict go away.

Here, then, is the version of speciesism that, unlike (5), coheres with liberationism and can also digest the most compelling speciesist intuitions:

> Speciesism (6): Human interests are more important than animal interests, in the sense that promoting even trivial human interests ought to take precedence over advancing animal interests. Only survival interests justify actively thwarting an animal's survival interests.

While (6) is intuitive, (5) is not. Strategically, the advantage of endorsing (6) from a liberationist stance is that the most counterintuitive implications of liberationism, on which antiliberationists focus, become conceptually dissociated from liberationism. One can obviously choose to hold on to them too, maintaining that survival conflicts do not justify sacrificing animals. But liberationism as such does not require this fraught extension.

My goal is *not* to urge liberationists to begin defining themselves as speciesists. My aim is to show that the category of "speciesism" is itself not important: accepting or denying that one is or is not a speciesist, at least in most of its senses, does not have much of a bearing on the issues that are actually debated and on the practices that need to be abolished. Moreover, the more popular speciesist intuitions can be readily digested by liberationists without jeopardizing the call for reform. Later chapters in this book show how this modified liberationist argument mobilizes criticism of specific animal-related practices.

Chapter 2

WHY ANIMALS MATTER

VIRTUALLY ALL WORK IN ANIMAL ETHICS attempts to establish or reform the "moral status" of nonhuman animals. I will argue that for all its importance, such work introduces confusion into animal ethics that in turn carries significant ramifications. I will first give a rough outline of status-establishing theories within animal ethics. I shall then argue that we can safely eliminate the notion of status, preserving what is of value in previous work. I will also outline the general assumptions that are sufficient for determining the moral standing of animal-related practices. Fortunately, these assumptions are widely shared.

Two-Stage Theories

Animal ethicists typically argue that animals possess "moral status." Such status is then supposed to underlie particular entitlements for animals. Under the rights view, upgrading status can secure animals genuine rights. We can call such approaches "two-stage" theories (stage 1: establish "moral status"; stage 2: generate moral prohibitions on animal-related conduct based on the "status" secured at stage 1). Notions and constructions such as "moral considerability," "moral entitlement," "exclusion," "inclusion," "moral status," or "moral patienthood" constitute interchangeable terms through which two-stage theories are articulated. The utilitarian version of a two-stage theory establishes moral entitlement via pain-pleasure awareness or through the capacity to satisfy or frustrate an animal's (nonlinguistic) interests or preferences. After establishing moral status in this way, the theory places conduct restrictions relating to pain, interests, or preferences. Rights-based two-stage theories reject the viability of a selective (speciesist) ascription of rights. After grounding animal rights in this way, the rights theorist will formulate limitations on conduct issuing from some account of welfare constituents that ought to be respected in any being that possesses rights.

Common to all two-stage theories is the premise that some actions ought not be done to animals *because* they possess moral status. The assumption that moral glue binds moral status with conduct is perhaps natural. Yet what is "moral status"? When one scrutinizes this frequently used construction, it appears to mean nothing more than protection: entities possessing "some degree" of "moral status" are entities to which some actions should not be done. Note, though, that this last sentence pinpoints semantic equivalence, *not* logical entailment. It is not the case that morally undesirable actions ought not be done *because* the being "has" or "possesses" moral status. Rather, beings possessing moral status *are* beings to which some actions ought not be done on moral grounds. The interchangeability of status with limitations on conduct is readily perceived when one attempts to (impossibly) define moral status through terms that are irreducible to protection. Moral status is *not* a necessary and sufficient condition for moral protection; moral status *just is* moral protection. Put another way, nothing is lost if one admits that many actions ought not be done to an entity, rather than contending that the entity "possesses" moral status and "therefore" is not to be maltreated.

I shall soon claim that we are not merely splitting hairs and that noting this subtlety early on prevents us from paying high prices later. Yet I first need to explain why moral status has been introduced into animal ethics literature in the first place. There are two sources for this, and the first is clear enough. Opponents of animal reform have rejected extending moral protection to animals by *inversing* the two-stage move above: they claimed that animals ought not be morally protected *because* they lack moral status. And so while a two-stage response on behalf of animals was misguided, it was a natural rejoinder given the misleading parameters of the debate. The second reason for adopting this obfuscating framework stems from misleading established uses of "status." Take citizenship. John is entitled to enter his country without a visa because he is a citizen of that country. John's status (citizenship) here designates properties that he has. Animals appear to resemble this example. They possess properties that are deemed morally relevant, entailing moral restrictions on conduct in relation to them. The mistake here relates to missing a distinction between two distinct relations between properties and the conduct entitlements with which they are linked. Some relations involve an intermediary stage of establishing status that then generates rights or restrictions. Other relations do not involve this mediating step. John's daughter becomes a citizen by exemplifying a relevant property (being the daughter of another citizen) and is then allowed to enter her country without a visa. On the other hand, a person who is, for example, kind, elicits a certain response from others (for example, respect) not because exemplifying kindness establishes some status (which then, in turn, induces respect). Kindness *calls* for respect, and explaining this need not appeal to some mediating "status" attained by exercising benevolent conduct.

Why does this imperceptibly minor point matter? The most obvious gain of replacing the vocabulary of moral considerability with that of moral restrictions is that we begin from consensual premises: some animal-related conduct is immoral.[1] Sadists aside, it is universally acknowledged that some actions ought not be done to animals. Anticruelty laws that exist in many countries dress this sentiment in legal trappings, and various religions manifest concern over limiting pain suffered by animals. Ethical committees authorizing scientific experiments aim to ensure that the pain experienced by animals is minimized, and that the least number of animals is being used. My claim is not that the present status quo is morally satisfying, but that it encapsulates the realization that animals are entitled to some moral defense, that it is universally recognized that something in animals calls for morally restricting what may be done to them.

Of course, a majority of people would prohibit only a few animal-related actions—for most such restriction typically consists in disallowing cruelty—and this means that moral philosophizing that challenges the present practices should strive to enlarge the set of banned actions. Such extension is possible without invoking the notion of moral status, or adopting utilitarianism, or arguing that animals have rights. Two-stage thinking is to be abandoned. But fortunately, this does not mean that all the incisive work into moral considerability in the last three decades is valueless. I will now offer a broad distinction between two kinds of status-establishing arguments. I will then say what may be retained from such moves if we discard the vocabulary of moral status.

Positive and Negative Arguments

Liberationists offer two kinds of status-establishing arguments. I will call these "positive" and "negative" arguments, respectively. A "positive" case for the moral considerability of animals isolates properties that animals have, making them eligible for substantial moral status. In highlighting particular properties—e.g., the capacity to suffer, feel, or think—positive arguments relate to content that either underlies or ought to underlie moral entitlement. "Negative" pro-animal arguments, on the other hand, undermine attempts to deny to animals considerable moral entitlement. Negative arguments do not ask what morally relevant properties animals possess, but challenge opponents of pro-animal reform to specify the morally relevant properties that animals *lack*. Negative

---

[1] For a different approach that starts off from this premise, see M. Rowland, *Animals Like Us* (London: Verso, 2002).

arguments concern form, not content. They do not harp on this or that property. Instead, such arguments first denaturalize the assumption that substantial moral status includes humans alone. Negative moves enforce a rethinking of this grouping principle (an undertheorized principle in traditional moral philosophy). Negative arguments are not primarily about human/nonhuman similarities. They underscore arbitrary exclusion.

Take, for example, the appeal to animal rights.[2] A "positive" variant of the rights argument is a case for the moral considerability of animals that, in turn, gives rise to rights. A negative version is that animals are eligible for substantive moral considerability if no morally relevant difference between human and nonhuman animals can explain why rights ought to be confined to humans. Appealing to species membership cannot suffice on its own (intelligent aliens obviously call for moral defense, and this shows that species membership is parasitical upon other morally relevant properties, in this case intelligence). Yet (the rights argument proceeds), humans with severe mental disabilities can be cognitively and emotionally inferior to some animals. Ergo, if the latter properties guarantee rights, humans cannot be the only ones who justifiably possess them.

Appealing to rights can constitute, in this sense, a "negative" case for moral considerability: it will not clarify the positive basis for bestowing rights but will expose the lack of a defensible principle for exclusion. The argument did not state or rely on intelligence being a morally relevant property. It merely placed the burden of proof on opponents of the animal case, challenging them to specify a property that humans exclusively possess, that can justify excluding rights to animals. After showing that species membership cannot suffice, the animal advocate eliminates possible candidates (such as the possession of intelligence) that can potentially vindicate the exclusion of animals. Rights-talk can consequently function as a roundabout tool through which moral considerability is established.[3]

---

[2] Actual rights advocates typically combine what I call negative and positive arguments. My focus here is on the general argumentative routes proposed by the literature. I shall accordingly avoid discussing the contours of particular distinct positions. For elaborate animal rights arguments, see Cavalieri, *The Animal Question*; Regan, *The Case for Animals Rights*; and S. V. Wise, *Rattling the Cage: Towards Legal Rights for Animals* (London: Profile Books, 2001).

[3] This is as good a place as any to spell out my discomfort with the rights argument as such. The pull to a rights-based view has clear advantages: first, rights are a standard legal tool through which moral prescriptions are soldered to conduct. If some or all animals have certain rights, reform becomes mandatory. Rights are also familiar entities in moral and legal discourse, and invoking them clarifies not only the "why" of reform, but also the "how" of it: animal rights advocates seek to broaden the application of a well-known concept. The case for animal rights thus becomes politically radical and at the same time philosophically conservative: one is relying on a familiar moral conceptual apparatus in order to establish unfamiliar political results. And yet, a central problem with the rights argument is

By contrast, positive arguments for moral inclusion delineate and defend specific morally relevant properties. Pro-animal utilitarians, for example, contend that the capacity to suffer makes animals worthy of direct moral concern. Alternatively, for Bernard Rollin, having things *matter* to an entity is a sufficient condition for inclusion. These answers are interconnected: if a being suffers, then things matter to it (minimally, the avoidance of pain matters to it, that is, the being is not indifferent to pain). Similarly, possessing interests seems inseparable from some relationship with pain/pleasure.[4] From a liberationist perspective, Rollin's answer is somewhat more inclusive than the hedonic utilitarian variant, since it covers behavior of animals such as fish and crabs, in which some have doubted the existence of pain.[5] Moreover, when mobilizing reform, Rollin's underscoring of interests (rather than pain alone) entails opposing not only practices that induce pain, but also practices involving significant thwarting of the interests of animals, a difference that will become more significant later in this book. Notwithstanding these differences, the Rollin-Bentham view on moral standing is intuitive: entities that care about what happens to them, even when such care is non-linguistic, are obvious candidates for inclusion. This view also clarifies why actions directed at animals differ from those done to vegetables or

---

the gap between sharing all non-species-related morally relevant properties and the eligibility for rights. It is coherent to claim that while A and B have the same morally relevant properties (say that A is human with a severe mental disability and B is an intelligent chimpanzee), A possesses rights whereas B does not. The reason for this gap is that rights are only contingently dependent on the intrinsic properties of beings. Rights can and do relate to self-serving concerns (one wants to maintain moral and legal protection in case of serious injury to self or kin), or projections regarding the world in which one wants to live (in terms of extension of sympathy to dependent humans), or slippery-slope concerns relating to undesirable consequences if rights are not extended to injured humans. Concerns such as these can logically and practically be limited to humans even if some animals are not cognitively or emotionally inferior to them. Showing that some animals share the morally relevant intrinsic properties of some humans can then be beside the point, as such would not establish eligibility for rights.

[4] Though I will argue for a broader view, in which interests can be dissociated from pain-pleasure, thus opening the door to "inferior" animals in which some have doubted the existence of pain and pleasure. Seeing pain/pleasure awareness as a prerequisite for having interests is how Singer interprets Bentham in a piece published in *The New York Review of Books* (1990), cited in Cavalieri, *The Animal Question*, 62. Unlike Singer's explicit utilitarianism in *Animal Liberation* and subsequent publications, I do not know whether Rollin would accept the affiliation with utilitarianism that I am here ascribing to him. For Rollin's position see his *Animal Rights and Human Morality* (Buffalo, NY: Promtheus Books, 1981).

[5] The prerequisite that these answers set for having moral standing should be thought of as a sufficient though not a necessary condition: comatose individuals have moral standing without necessarily feeling pain or caring about what happens to them.

inanimate objects (or, for that matter, bacteria), thereby distinguishing animal ethics from other ecological moral concerns.

For all its immediate appeal, the Rollin-Bentham view can be challenged, as Frey did, through asking for its argumentative support. What argument, Frey asks, can substantiate the idea that when things matter to an entity, it is worthy of moral consideration?[6] One can also ask what makes the Rollin-Bentham view preferable to other theories of entitlement. What, for example, makes the connection between feeling pain and possessing moral standing more plausible than the Kantian conviction that only beings that can act not merely from laws but from thinking about these laws—which, on Kant's terminology, makes them possessors of "reason"—have direct moral standing (in Kant's terminology: such beings are "persons" rather than "things")? What makes the Bentham-Rollin view more acceptable than assuming that only language-possessing beings have interests, and, in turn, that only entities with interests possess moral standing? What makes this view superior to holding that moral standing is restricted to beings that can potentially actively participate in a hypothetical pact cast behind a veil of ignorance in order to legislate just moral laws, or to the view that entitlements arise from capabilities?

Although I claim that two-stage thinking is misguided, I will say why the Bentham-Rollin view is more plausible than these other two-stage moves since there is a component of this thinking that I will keep. A's capacity to feel pain means not merely that I can substantially affect A's life, but that I can make A's world very bad for A. I can obviously affect B's capacity to speak, frustrate B's interests, or prevent B from expressing his interests in the initial contracting stage. But if we do not *also* assume that these actions *cause* B to suffer, or if we do not also assume that they matter to B, the moral status of my actions remains unclear.[7] The rivals listed above to the Rollin-Bentham view are no alternatives; they *presuppose* it. We think that rational beings or language-possessing beings are entitled to moral standing *because* we tacitly assume that they can be affected by actions that matter to them. When these capacities are disconnected from the ability to suffer—imagine a race of rational, language-possessing aliens that are genuinely indifferent to actions that affect them—the ethical status of actions that are done in relation to the bearers of such

[6] See R. G. Frey, *Interests and Rights: The Case against Animals* (Oxford: Clarendon Press, 1980), chap. 11.

[7] That a comatose patient can be treated in morally wrong ways without a capacity to suffer or without such actions mattering to the patient is no counterexample here. The moral reasons against doing so differ from reasons against maltreating individuals that are capable of negative experiences.

capacities becomes mysterious.[8] The capacity for negative experience is not merely an additional factor working alongside other properties (e.g., possessing language). Language-possessing, rationality, etc.—when envisaged as status-endowing properties—all *imply* a capacity for negative experience, which is why it is *this* capacity that is doing the work in all theories of entitlement.

The Rollin-Bentham view is deeper than its alternatives ("deeper" in the sense that they presuppose it) and is to be preferred as an explication of the property by virtue of which an entity is worthy of moral concern.[9] This view is incomplete, since, in the framework of two-stage approaches, I presented it as offering a sufficient (though not a necessary) condition for entitlement to direct moral concern, or at the very least as being implied by a reason-based criteria for entitlement. But it forms a necessary part of a complete theory of such entitlement, and so this incompleteness need not bother those who argue for ascribing moral status to animals.

Exclusion Revisited

If two-stage thinking is wrong, why should we trouble over details that should only matter to others? The reason relates not to status, but to unpacking the meaning of "morally relevant properties," a construction I left as an unanalyzed primitive above. I denied that entities—human or nonhuman—"have" moral status. Instead, I claimed that they possess morally relevant properties that, in turn, morally restrict what may be done to them. I am accordingly obligated to elucidate what such properties are, as well as to face the possibility that some of these properties (for

---

[8] It is still probably impermissible to hurt such aliens. But such prohibition stems from either (a) an inability to imagine a genuine indifference (since in the world which we know, actions imply positive and negative preferences); (b) a belief that their Stoicism is a mistake; or (c) a general aversion to destructive action that covers objects as well as indifferent aliens (a Schweitzerian outlook according to which entities exemplify distinct and irreducible value that should not be affected). In our context, the first two possibilities are beside the point, as they do not really deal with a genuine possibility for a rational yet indifferent being. The third possibility, the Schweitzerian outlook, immediately plays into the hands of pro-animal advocates: a general ethical prescription of nonviolence undermines animal-related conduct that causes pain and death.

[9] For a different variant of this argument—Singer's claim that Nussbaum's capabilities approach, with regard to animals, presupposed utilitarian considerations—see his "A Response to Martha Nussbaum" (http://www.utilitarian.net/singer/by/20021113.htm). I will ignore possible criticisms from a more inclusive ecological perspective, according to which my focus on the capacity for negative experience shuts the door to many nonliving entities that should be counted as moral patients. Unlike attempts to narrow down inclusion, broader accounts of entitlement will have no quarrel with my conclusions regarding animals.

instance, the capacity to assent to moral rules or have linguistically formulated interests) are more important than others (e.g., the capacity to
undergo negative experiences).

We can afford to leave unaddressed the latter possibility since relative
importance of morally relevant properties does not affect any of the
practical conclusions that this book advances. As for explaining what
"morally relevant property" means, I can do no better than give a circu-
lar answer: P is a morally relevant property, if and only if the possession
of P by entity E calls for moral restrictions on actions that concern E. The
philosophically interesting question is why some properties are grouped
together as morally relevant while others are not. I do not know of good
answers to this question.[10] Yet if my argument in support of the Rollin-
Bentham position is sound, it appears that all of the known proposed
contenders for morally relevant properties have *either focused on or
presupposed* the capacity for negative experience. This suggests that the
capacity for negative experience either underlies other properties that because of it become morally relevant, or plays a different decisive role in
the core perceptions that guide our moral relations with others. The precise role of the capacity for negative experience in determining moral
relevancy can be left open. It is sufficient to recognize that the role is a
central one, and that animals clearly exemplify this capacity.[11]

[10] Kant gave a conditional answer to this question in the *Grundlegung*: *if* anything is to
have value, then one must grant unconditional value to the beings doing the evaluating.
Kant's answer is weak even if one is willing to grant that things (actions, states, objects) possess value (which nihilists would not). There is no contradiction in perceiving all value to be
merely conditional. Kant's argument is accordingly merely an assertion of the intrinsic value
of humans. Mill and Aristotle simply began with observable preferences, without asking
what makes these morally relevant properties. I am not aware of better answers in contemporary writings. DeGrazia (*Taking Animals Seriously*, 39–41) argues that interests are
morally relevant properties and that animals have them. Yet he does not enter the general
question regarding why some properties are relevant while others are not. For Cavalieri's
attempt to answer this question—leading to his own version of an experiential criteria—see
The Animal Question, 34. For a book-length argument in support of an experiential basis
for moral considerability, see M. H. Bernstein, *On Moral Considerability: An Essay on
Who Morally Matters* (Oxford: Oxford University Press, 1998).

[11] Apart from saying why it is preferable over alternatives, I raised Frey's concern regarding the argumentative basis of associating pain and entitlement with direct moral consideration. But if the Rollin-Bentham view does underlie other theories of entitlement, Frey's
challenge questions all plausible candidates for a theory of moral entitlement and can only
be circularly answered by a general conception of ethics. Here is a short version of such a
reply to Frey: If I am right about all theories of entitlement as presupposing the Rollin-
Bentham view, ethics is an attempt to formulate and organize the conduct that ought to hold
between entities that care about what happens to them. Some of these entities (humans) can
understand this attempt and be potentially motivated by its prescriptions. A smaller group of
these is actually motivated by these prescriptions. Such characterization of ethics can be understood descriptively (as capturing what ethics is) or nondescriptively (as articulating what

Going beyond two-stage thinking involves revising two-stage arguments into one-stage negative ones. For example, avoiding causing unnecessary suffering cannot be limited to human suffering. What moral reason can prevent extending the disinclination to create pain to suffering beings that, let us suppose, do not have rights, or have inferior cognitive and emotional capacities? Many aspects of pro-animal reform can be integrated into similar questions without establishing a positive case for moral considerability. Exploitation, killing (painless or not), or severe limitation of movement is either ruled out or requires extraordinary vindications when applied to human animals. Why should such limitations disappear when considering animals? These are negative arguments. They demand specifying what it is that animals lack that validates treating them in ways that are objectionable when directed at humans.

The familiar answer here is that the property that animals miss is "moral status" (adding that this is why it is fallacious to draw analogies between humans and animals: the latter "possess" status while the former do not, or the latter have "much more" of "it"). The original Cartesian elimination of the moral status of animals was predicated on an exclusively human mind-body dualism coupled with a denial of animal pain. A contemporary Cartesian will discard most or all aspects of the older position (the most important of which relates to pain: no one doubts the reality of animal pain), and will instead refuse granting moral considerability to animals until a positive case for such is established. Such a move—in effect shifting the burden of proof to the pro-animal advocate—is, in my impression, a common reaction of ethicists and other philosophers who are outside the animal debate. The problem with contemporary Cartesianism surfaces when trying to explain why some animal-related acts—say, manifestly cruel acts—ought to be prevented. Denying animals any moral considerability cannot cohere with morally restricting any animal-related conduct. Why should *any* conduct be considered abusive if animals have no moral status at all? Since even neo-Cartesians wish to eliminate sadism to animals, they will be hard-pressed to explain why and how such limitations on cruelty can be defended. Our neo-Cartesian will turn out to be, in effect, a neo-Kantian, defending some variety of a direct/indirect approach.

---

ethics should mean). When understood descriptively, Frey's challenge is beside the point as it seeks arguments where the sole question is of description and misdescription: associating pain and entitlement *is* simply the fundamental relation from which ethics begins. We know that our actions affect others; we know that they care about what we do; we then ask when such actions are justified and unjustified and what principles, if there are such, govern such justifications. This *is* how ethical thought begins. When understood nondescriptively, associating pain and entitlement *ought* to be preferred over its alternatives because it picks out the deepest property that does the actual work in all theories of moral entitlement.

Direct/indirect approaches attempt to prohibit some animal-related conduct without ascribing to animals moral status. The underlying idea is that cruelty to animals is to be prevented, and this is occasioned not by any property of the animals, but because of the concern *of* other (animal-loving) humans, or because of the concern *to* other humans (the projected threat being that cruelty to animals prompts cruelty to humans), or a concern for some ideal of humanity that is disrupted if cruelty to animals is allowed. The original formulation of this view in Kant's *Lectures on Ethics* includes the latter two aspects along with the pre-Darwinian teleological view of animals as means for humans. Peter Carruthers, a contemporary Kantian (though he may well disapprove of this title), argues against cruelty to animals through the first two considerations above: hurting the feelings of animal-loving humans, and the possibility that such cruelty will evolve into cruelty to humans. For Carruthers, there is nothing objectionable in cruelty to animals as such, if one is sure that none of these future undesirable consequences for humans will occur. (Carruthers's example in his *The Animal Issue* is of a scientist that leaves Earth on a spaceship and desires to torture her cat. In Carruthers's opinion, such torture is morally unproblematic, so long as others never hear about it.)

The weakness in indirect theories is that the specific animal-related actions that they ban can be substantially extended by utilizing negative arguments. Take Kant's desire to banish cruelty not because it is a wrong done to the animal, but because cruelty makes for a warped humanity. If a desired ideal of humanity is disrupted by malicious behavior to animals, why stop at manifest cruelty, rather than target avoidable hidden and institutionalized activities that cause suffering? Alternatively, if one concedes, as Kant did, that cruelty to animals can lead to cruelty to people, supposing (precariously) that some causal or didactic link exists between animal-related conduct and actions that are directed at humans, it seems plausible to hold that a further deepening of kindness extended to animals may well be a springboard to more general tendencies to nonviolence with regard to other humans.[12] I have read no one who unequivocally

---

[12] Like most causal claims regarding moral education, I do not think that a deeper recognition of animal exploitation will necessarily lead to a kinder outlook on people. Pacifist tendencies in Indian culture are sometimes associated with widespread vegetarianism. Yet this linkage strikes me as dubious since India also suffers from systematic violence between casts, some of which are strictly vegetarian. We also know that the Third Reich developed one of the most progressive outlooks on animals without any marked spillover effect from this to diminish the sufferings of humans. If deeper concern for animals is supposed to encourage better relations with people, it is only one ingredient in a moral education, and even then, like any good education, no guarantee exists for success. But the negative argument for considerability need not prove such causal connections. The

asserts that cruelty to animals should be prevented solely because of the
feelings of animal lovers (Carruthers comes close). Yet if someone concedes that such feelings are a sufficient reason to prevent some conduct,
then (again) such feelings should encourage us to question other practices
with relation to animals. To conclude: limiting some animal-related actions because of moral concerns can cohere with a denial of the moral
considerability of animals (if we must use the notion of considerability at
all), but it opens the door to pro-animal extension of morally unaccept-
able animal-related conduct.

Kant himself did not foresee such extension, since, like Aristotle and
Aquinas, Kant endorsed the teleological (and sometimes theological)
view that animals are means for human ends. Kant also distinguished between persons and objects through identifying persons with entities who
can reason (according to his particular understanding of "reasoning").
Can such an anthropocentric position be reformulated in credible terms
in contemporary bioethics? A modernized secularized neo-Kantianism
will avoid teleology and will retain some linkage between reasoning and
moral status. A neo-Kantian of this type will then contend that animals
can never be wronged because they are not the kind of entities that can
be wronged. To distinguish between entities that can and cannot be
wronged, the neo-Kantian will appeal to a particular capacity to reason
that is peculiar to humans. To avoid the apparently obtuse ramifications
that this reasoning carries for humans that exhibit diminished reasoning
capacities, the neo-Kantian will appeal to a kind-token framework: humans are the kind of being that can be wronged, so individual humans
that lose the capacity to reason (or will never attain it) preserve rights because they belong to this kind. Animals, on the other hand, belong to the
kind of being that cannot be wronged, regardless of the capacity of a
small number of them to surpass some humans.[13]

---

argument merely challenges a defender of the Kantian position, who *does* endorse some
version of the causal thesis, to clarify why it is plausible to stop at preventing cruelty, given
her belief in some connection between animal-related and human related practice.

[13] See Carl Cohen, "The Case for the Use of Animals in Biomedical Research," originally
published in the *New England Journal of Medicine* 315 (14) (1986): 865–69, now also
available at http://www.ucalgary.ca/~powlesla/personal/hunting/rights/cohen.txt: "Persons
who are unable, because of some disability, to perform the full moral functions natural to
human beings are certainly not for that reason ejected from the moral community. The
issue is one of kind. Humans are of such a kind that they may be the subject of experiments
only with their voluntary consent. The choices they make freely must be respected. Animals
are of such a kind that it is impossible for them, in principle, to give or withhold voluntary
consent or to make a moral choice. What humans retain when disabled, animals have never
had." For criticism of Cohen's argument, see Cavalieri, *The Animal Question*, 77–78.
Cavalieri argues that no substantive differentiating content can be given to the notions of

If a being is wronged, it is (usually) also harmed. Yet the Kantian says that a being (a nonhuman animal) can be harmed (put in pain, for example), without being wronged. I argued above that a reason-biased foundation for moral considerability presupposes—rather than competes with—an experiential account: we regard reasoning entities as morally significant because we *also* know that such beings can be affected in ways that matter to them. I said that it is the ability to be harmed (rather than to reason) that does the underlying moral work. Reasoning beings can be harmed—"harm" covering more than negative experience, extending to various deprivations that need not be experienced as losses—and since the capacity to be harmed in these ways is a property that animals share too, moral conduct restrictions ought to cover them. My neo-Kantian critic will now claim that my argument is beside the point: that I am misunderstanding the distinction between being harmed and being wronged. The neo-Kantian agrees that humans and nonhumans can both be harmed, but that only in humans can such harm be (sometimes) wrong, and this uniqueness of humans stems from their particular capacity to reason in a certain way.

In arguing against this variant of neo-Kantianism I will avoid the empirical claims within pro-animal literature that are designed to undermine the association of animals with nonreasoning entities.[14] Nor will I revisit the conceptual difficulties of showing that a distinguishing property (in our case, the capacity to reason in a highly articulate way) is also a (or the only) morally relevant one. Instead I wish to point out some dubious implications of neo-Kantianism. First, by appealing to a kind-token framework, the neo-Kantian cannot avoid endorsing an offending outlook regarding mentally disabled human beings: these cannot be wronged by virtue of what they are, but because they happen to belong

---

"kind" or "human nature" that underlie Cohen's move. For other critical discussions of Cohen, see DeGrazia, *Taking Animals Seriously*, 3637; and Nathan Nobis, "Carl Cohen's 'Kind' Argument for Animal Rights and Against Human Rights," *Journal of Applied Philosophy* 21 (1) (2004): 43–59. For a different kind-token response to the problem of marginal cases, this time cast in terms of the greater value of human lives, see W. Patton, "Vivisection, Morals, Medicine: Commentary from a Vivisecting Professor of Pharmacology," *Journal of Medical Ethics* 9 (2) (1983): 102–4.

[14] For attempts to undermine such association, see some of the chapters of S. F. Sapontzis, *Morals, Reason, and Animals* (Philadelphia: Temple University Press, 1987); Regan, *The Case for Animal Rights*, chap. 2; and ongoing work by Mark Berkoff. Relevant too are many chapters in Rosemary Rodd's *Biology, Ethics and Animals* (Oxford: Clarendon Press, 1990). Hebrew readers will greatly profit from Ze'ev Levy and Nadav Levy, *Ethics, Emotions and Animals: On the Moral Status of Animals* (Haifa: Sifriat Poalim and University of Haifa Press, 2002).

to the right kind. The capacity of disabled individuals to be happy, be comfortable, experience severe pain, or have their interests frustrated—all count for nothing. Such an implication would appall anyone who is familiar with such individuals or their families, or is concerned about developing a moral and political philosophy that can adequately respond to and accommodate disabled individuals rather than perceive them as having some derivative standing.

Second, neo-Kantianism implies the alarming thought that the moral status of us humans is contingent upon our intellectual capacities; should these universally drop (say that some unforeseen ecological factor will dramatically dumb down all humans), we become morally free game. Suppose, for example, that humans retain some capacity for communication, some social organization, but no ability (actual or potential) to read or write, not to mention an ability to understand Kant's moral writings. For the neo-Kantian it would follow that for a race of moral aliens that would visit Earth ("moral" in the sense that, unlike us humans, these aliens do understand and follow Kantian morality, "follow" in the minimal sense of them endowing value to actions, and realizing that moral prescriptions are universal), there will be no moral objection preventing them from treating us in any way they like.

Third, the neo-Kantian's distinction between being harmed and being wronged is itself misleading. True, examples such as warfare and self-defense show that entities can be severely harmed without being wronged. But the requirement to justify the infliction of harm indicates that harming is a prima facie wrong. Harm cannot thus be cleanly divorced from moral components as the Kantian hopes. The Kantian will retort that harm is a prima facie wrong only when directed at other humans. But this claim flies in the face of widely shared agreement—exhibited in slaughter codes, hunting norms, the "triple R" restriction on vivisection—according to which minimizing the harm done to animals is a goal that ought to be pursued. The obligation to excuse inflicting harm does not seem to be species bound.

Fourth, the Kantian's appeal to a notion of humanity that one distorts if one is cruel to animals seems to smuggle through the backdoor a tacit recognition that animals can be wronged (rather than merely "harmed"). Why else should cruel acts make for a flawed humanity if animals are morally neutral entities? Think of tables or chairs. Such objects can be destroyed or damaged. Yet nothing one does to such objects indicates undesirable humanity. Aside from examples within environmental ethics, we do not usually regard object-related conduct as potentially determining our humanity in a negative way. We would accordingly be puzzled to learn that animal-related conduct was such a determining factor. Kant's talk of animal-related misconduct as speaking poorly for us relies then on an implicit recognition within his readers, according to which animals can be the subjects of immoral conduct.[15]

BEYOND TWO-STAGE THEORIES

Neo-Kantianism is indefensible. "Denying" animals "moral status" cannot be maintained. This does not mean that animals—or humans for that matter—"have" moral status or that animal-related conduct reform needs to await the "establishment" of moral status for them. Instead, the liberationist merely claims that some actions ought not be done to animals. The reason for this restriction is that animals are entities that can be harmed, and there is a moral obligation to avoid harming unless a solid justification is provided (for an unpacking of "solid," see below). Single-stage thinking absorbs from previous theorists the refutation of attempts to exclude animals from any moral concern. Single-stage thinking also deploys the force of negative arguments (without invoking rights): demanding specification of the property that animals lack which could vindicate thwarting their interests in distinct ways. Finally, single-stage thinking utilizes the utilitarian delineation of morally relevant properties (without adopting an overall utilitarian approach). Given the inability to justifiably ostracize animals from the pale of moral thought, no philosophical barrier prevents reforming animal-related conduct: minimizing pain whenever possible, attempting to coexist with animals in nonexploitative ways, and, in general, endorsing a hands-off approach.[16]

Liberationists might worry that in this deflation of the argument in favor of reform, we end up with overly lean moral operators. Theoretical minimization is usually a virtue. Yet in the animal context, the remaining framework must be substantial, capable of mobilizing controversial moral

---

[15] In his *Created from Animals: The Moral Implications of Darwinism* (Oxford: Oxford University Press, 1990), James Rachels offered a different argument against the kind-token framework, claiming that endorsing it entails (unintuitively) that a highly intelligent ape or rodent (say, one who can discuss philosophy) is still an adequate candidate for experimentation simply because it belongs to the wrong kind. The difficulty I have with this move is that it is not obvious to me that rats that write philosophy books remain rats (is Kafka's Gregor Samsa simply an overgrown insect?). And if philosophy writing is a property that sufficiently disrupts the kind-categorization (as surely some properties would), Rachel's argument fails.

[16] I will not enter the question of positive obligations with regard to animals, obligations that may qualify what "hands off" should morally mean. For such discussion, see Martha Nussbaum, *Frontiers of Justice: Disability, Nationality, Species Membership* (Cambridge: Harvard University Press, 2006), 372–80. Later chapters in this book restrict the desirability of the "hands-off" objective in terms of the overall good of animals. In sum, I argue that letting animals be is a liberationist value, though not an overriding one.

prescriptions and dislodging deeply engrained practices. The rights approach or utilitarianism provide sufficient machinery for this purpose: if animals possess rights, then some weighty conduct reform is called for. Reforms follow too, if the hedonic calculus determining the overall pleasure and pain (which, according to utilitarians, should guide our actions) includes animals. Liberationists would worry that when compared to rights or utilitarian-based approaches, the negative arguments proposed earlier as sufficient lack theoretic force. The problem is not merely that such arguments are eclectically assembled in the sense of being unrelated to an overall principled theory, but that they carry little probative force when clashing against opposing and diverse antireform human interests. In absence of rights or an overall moral theory like utilitarianism, the problem becomes one of balancing moral limitations on conduct against considerations that many regard as more powerful and that tap interests that are closer to home.

Consider severe limitation of movement. Restricting movement calls for a justification when it is applied to another human. Since we have no reason to suppose that animals do not experience severe limitation of movement as a harm, we need to ask what it is that animals lack that legitimates limiting their movement (a "negative argument" according to the typology proposed above). In the case of some companion animals, the justification will appeal to the animal's own welfare and the quasi-paternalistic framework of pet-owner relations that may support such restriction. Some companion animals would never exist in the wild, and so placing them outside the confines of a human home would be detrimental to them. Caging birds, on the other hand, does not admit of similar excuse; nor does the capture of animals that live in the wild, to put them on display in zoos. Suppose now that a defender of zoos admits that the institution is morally dubious, but that the pleasure for numerous visitors offsets the moral transgression done to animals. Parallel formulations exist regarding other areas of animal welfare. Killing animals as part of scientific enquiry, diet, hunting, and the clothing industry can all appear undesirable as such, but as minor wrongs in comparison with the human interests that are being promoted. The more ambitious theories to which I am proposing a thinner alternative contain handy dismissals of such appeals: if animals have rights, or if their interests or suffering are part of the overall morally relevant state of affairs that ought to guide utilitarian decision making, the construction "trumping human interest" encounters substantial counterarguments. Rights cannot be easily "trumped" (indeed, that is what sets rights apart from mere interests). As for the utilitarian framework, "human interest"—even if the utilitarian perceives "human interest" as more important than the interests of animals—will be quantified and set against the severe disutility to animals that all of the above practices involve. The result would most probably suggest that the examined practice needs to be eradicated.

How, then, does a nonutilitarian, non-rights-based approach respond to someone saying that product safety, the advancement of science, or mere human pleasure overrides even intense harm done to animals? Specific responses will be taken up in following chapters. But it is important to acknowledge from the start, that no response we can make can appease an opponent that insists on such claims. Like other areas within ethics, basic assumptions, preferences, and sensitivities cannot be conclusively proved. One cannot, for instance, *prove* that child molesting or rape is a wrong if the assumptions underlying this judgment are consistently called into question. Someone who, for example, genuinely refuses to see the child's potential suffering as offsetting the molester's intense pleasure cannot be corrected via logically compelling arguments that would enforce on him his mistake. Moral transformation in the past—banishing slavery or the social subordination of women to men—has required curtailing one group's privileges and pleasures relative to another. This process never involved (impossibly) *proving* that, say, a world that cultivates equality among men and women is morally superior to a patriarchal system, or that a slaveless world is manifestly better. The moral dimensions of such processes (setting aside the nonmoral factors) involved an intensifying sense of moral disharmony within a growing number of people, sensing that some forms of suffering or unequal treatment can no longer be justified, and that these call for change. Moral reform in such domains is less a matter of offering argument and more of creating and accommodating perception of hitherto unobserved suffering, or of facilitating a vivid grasp of wrongs that have been superficially rationalized away. Such denaturalization of time-honored customs and institutions in turn leads to their modification or replacement.

The role of philosophical argument in such a process is mostly limited to destabilization and refutation of the justificatory basis of the existing institutions. They show that certain deprivations and thwarting of interests cannot be upheld. They also appeal to internal coherence within one's moral perceptions and judgments, claiming that achieving such coherence entails reform. Finally, like abolitionism and feminism, animal liberationists try to create a fairer world, one in which avoidable suffering is reduced or eliminated. They cannot modify the thinking of someone who is genuinely unmoved by these sentiments and convictions. But in this regard, rights advocates and pro-animal utilitarians are not on firmer ground than single-stage thinking. Consistent antiliberationists can always insist that human interests override rights-possessing animals, or that these interests count for more than animal interests in a utilitarian calculus.[17]

To conclude, animals cannot be denied moral status. Yet this does not imply that they possess "it." Animals have morally relevant properties, properties, that is, that call for moral restrictions on what may be done to them. These properties include the capacity to be subjected to negative experience, and the capacity to be harmed even if such harm is not experienced. The recognition that animals exemplify such properties is intuitive, widely shared, and manifested in the consensual desire to eliminate cruelty to animals. Given such recognition, it is untenable to limit ourselves to rejecting only some forms of cruelty rather than striving to eliminate or diminish all forms of unnecessary suffering. Older forms of dismissal of animals that could justify limiting our concern to cruelty alone—Cartesian, Kantian—can no longer be validly summoned. This opens the door to abolishing or substantially reforming age old institutions. The moral case on behalf of animals is not stronger (though not weaker) than other large-scale moral reforms. It relies on intuitions, negative arguments, extension of existing moral convictions and sentiments, intensifying acknowledgment and perception of suffering, and deconstructing attempts to preserve the status quo. It is not a proof. Single-stage moves can guide reform in specific areas of animal welfare, and this will be undertaken in the more detailed discussions in this book.

[17] Animal ethicists would here note the influence of the books by Sapontzis and DeGrazia on my own approach. Both avoid nesting the claims on behalf of animals within broader theories. DeGrazia focuses on internal coherence and Sapontzis on minimizing pain and shifting the burden of proof onto those who would uphold exploitative practices. Both shun grander theories, preferring minimal starting points.

PART II

Killing

Chapter 3

KILLING FOR PLEASURE

IT IS USUALLY ASSUMED that moral vegetarians are obliged to prove a number of difficult claims. These include the claim that animals are not automata; that animals suffer or experience pain; that killing animals harms them; that killing or causing them pain matters to animals in a way that should make an ethical difference to us; that animals have some kind of moral status; that we have positive or negative obligations to nonhuman animals; or, more ambitiously, that animals possess rights that, in turn, call for these negative/positive obligations.

This way of framing the debate and its major stepping-stones has a strong hold on the philosophical literature on vegetarianism. Yet it is a misleading framework. The error lies in confusing between justifying widely shared beliefs and drawing the moral consequences that are plausibly implied by such beliefs *given* the fact that they are shared. The immorality of child-torture is, for example, predicated on a belief in the existence of other minds, the justification of which has been repeatedly contested. Yet since the belief in other minds is widely shared, the implication for moral action does not require a proof of this prior claim even if it happens to underlie it. By contrast, when the underlying beliefs are *not* shared, implications for action have to await a justification of these underlying beliefs (e.g., implications for abortion largely depend on contested beliefs regarding the moral and ontological status of the fetus). This confusion, as well as the attempt to ground vegetarianism on a broader theory of animal welfare, has led to adopting a misleading framework for this specific debate.

Distinguishing between beliefs held and beliefs proved can show where genuine disagreements between vegetarians and their opponents lie, and delineating these points is this chapter's first goal. Vegetarian and nonvegetarians will agree that there are some moral restrictions on our relations with animals. Anticruelty legislation and ethical supervision on animal experimentation within research institutes are indicative of this shared consensus. Animals should not, for example, be tortured or even painlessly killed for an insubstantial reason (think of someone who purchases hundreds of healthy cats and dogs just for the purpose of euthanizing them painlessly). Five nontrivial beliefs are implied by this shared condemnation, and it is important to note them since they are sometimes denied: first, a belief in a morally relevant difference between animals and objects: we are morally indifferent to people who slowly mince and shred their own furniture, smiling as they do so;[1] second, a belief in animal pain; third, a belief in the moral relevance of animal pain; fourth, a belief that there are cases in which such pain should trump even intense human pleasures (suppose that euthanizing the puppies gives the person intense pleasure); fifth, a belief that killing animals, painless or not, is a harm done to the killed animal, and that some justification for doing so is required.

Proving these beliefs is an important task. But disputants in the vegetarian debate make two mistakes: first they suppose that proving these is a burden that vegetarians need to carry alone; second, that vegetarians need to carry this burden at all. Why prove beliefs that everyone shares anyway?[2] Here the philosopher's urge to examine the supposedly obvious hampers moral clarity. The philosophers who are interested in animals will work hard to prove, say, why animal pain matters morally; they will in turn get challenged on these arguments by other philosophers, and the ensuing debate will create the mirage that the moral status of a contested aspect of the animal issue (here vegetarianism) *depends* on the validity of the proof of this anterior claim. Challenging a defender of vegetarianism to prove why painlessly killing an animal harms the animal is as plausible as demanding a feminist to solve the Other Minds problem. In one way both are reasonable requests: vegetarianism is predicated on a belief in the harm involved in animal death in much the same way that feminism is predicated on the assumption that other people exist. Philosophers are interested in the problematic basis for these latter assumptions. But at the same time these challenges are not to the point as proponents and opponents share the beliefs in question anyway. Justifying the condemnation

---

[1] Some objects, such as works of art, historical buildings, or natural objects, also give rise to moral restrictions regarding what may be done to them, though most theorists would agree that these restrictions are anthropocentrically derived. Unlike animals, in the case of objects some actions become wrong due to the concerns of actual or potential humans, not because they ought not be done to these objects. Nothing wrong is done *to* the object. Kant's attempt to apply this idea to animals via his famous direct/indirect duties distinction in his *Lectures on Ethics* was predicated on an identification of animals with means for human welfare, a teleological view going back at least to Aquinas, which has no contemporary defenders. Advocates of a nonanthropocentric view of objects within environmental ethics ("deep ecologists") will disagree with my point here but can still accept my general argument above.

[2] Note the difference between this argument and a close one presented by Andrew Tardiff in "Simplifying the Case for Vegetarianism," *Social Theory and Practice*, 22 (3) (1996): 299–314). Tardiff attempts to use intuitions elicited from similar thought experiments to argue for vegetarianism. I am distinguishing between proving, or arguing for a belief, and showing that it is held. I share Tardiff's belief that the vegetarian debate can and should be simplified, in the sense of detaching it from other issues and assumptions on which literature on animal welfare focuses.

of painless killing of animals is an important question, and I do not mean to shortcut it through this argument. My claim, up to this point, is not substantive but methodological (I am not, for example, claiming—yet— that accepting the five beliefs above necessitates adopting moral vegetarianism): *contesting the justifications* of beliefs is different from *rejecting* these beliefs. Put differently, the case for moral vegetarianism appeals to coherence within *existing* beliefs that are commonly held by nonvegetarians and then proceeds to claim that eating animals does not cohere with them.[3]

This distinction generates a typology of possible philosophical opponents of moral vegetarianism. To begin with, those who actually *reject* one or all of these beliefs (as opposed to contesting the justification of them) will also be rejecting vegetarianism. Deny that animals feel pain, and you are on your way to dismissing moral vegetarianism. Call this "antivegetarianism" as distinguished from "nonvegetarianism." An antivegetarian positively rejects one or more of the five assumptions above, while a nonvegetarian accepts them but does not see why they imply vegetarianism. These two opponents of vegetarianism should be distinguished from a third distinct opponent, whom I will call "the agnostic meat-eater." Unlike the antivegetarian, agnostic meat-eaters do not positively reject one of these fundamental assumptions, but, unlike nonvegetarians, they do not accept them either. Theirs is the position of those who await compelling arguments. They await persuasion that these beliefs are justified, and they see no reason to modify their diet until such a justification is produced. Agnostic meat-eaters would charge vegetarians for holding (but not proving) basic beliefs that underlie their case, say, the belief that killing is harmful for the killed entity, or that pain is bad for the sufferer. While they do not deny these claims, and may even credit them with initial plausibility, agnostic meat-eaters would say that we cannot simply take the vegetarian's word vouching for the truth of these, and that a supporting argument is therefore needed.

---

[3] Cf. Mark Rowlands's method in *Animals Like Us*, 28–31. An honorary title for this strategy is "an appeal to moral integrity." Fairness requires me to mention that the other name for such arguments is circumstantial ad hominem. The grand defense of employing such moves in philosophy is Johnston's: all philosophical arguments are of the circumstantial ad hominem kind. Henry W. Johnstone, Jr., *Validity and Rhetoric in Philosophical Argument: An Outlook in Transition* (University Park, PA: Dialogue Press of Man & World, 1978). But relying on circumstantial ad hominem arguments is defensible through routs that are more mundane. The fact that many logic textbooks classify such moves as "fallacies" means that, like any nonformal fallacies (for example, appeal to authority), only some applications of such moves can be accepted (appealing to a friend's authority when explaining why one takes a pill is implausible; appealing to a physician's authority is not). Aspects of the context usually determine the legitimacy of such moves, and in the context of the vegetarian debate I see nothing that makes the strategy flawed.

We now have a typology of dismissals of moral vegetarianism. Let us evaluate them in turn.

Antivegetarianism militates against too much common moral sense (the antivegetarian is, recall, *rejecting* one of the five assumptions above). Disagreement exists as to what constitutes adequate justification, but (as the euthanized puppies example shows) people do not believe that killing animals needs no justification whatsoever. It is also uncontested that some uses of animals constitute abuses of them and are to be prevented even when such restriction frustrates a strong human pleasure (e.g., sadistic pleasure). Denying that animals feel pain (or that they are responding but unfeeling automata and are thus objects) has also become unpopular in post-Cartesian bioethics: animals limp on hurt limbs, react to painful stimuli, have endorphin (even some worms produce it), and respond to pain-relieving medication. Saying that all this is "instinct" rather than "pain" as we know it in its human-articulated form is implausible since it implies, first, that babies' responses to painful stimuli are also "instinctive" rather than morally relevant pain, and second, that human pain is divorced from the domain of instinct, and something radically different is going on when humans and nonhuman animals are pricked by a needle.[4] Antivegetarians would have to work hard to unsettle such convictions, and it is difficult to imagine how they can do so.

An antivegetarian might deny that killing animals harms them, especially if it is done painlessly, and that it is thus not a wrong requiring justification. This too is implausible since the obligation to justify any killing of animals is shared across cultures and is at least as old as the

---

[4] There is a more plausible, selective version of this argument that denies the pain of "lower" animals, regarding these as no more than automata. Intuitively, I do not see much of a difference between a chicken and a crab, in terms of either death perception or the capacity to feel pain (I have my doubts about oysters, which strike me as thoroughly vegetative beings). After all, we have no means of verifying that more complex neurological systems make the pain experienced by and through them more intense for the organism. This is why the distinction between vertebrates and invertebrates strikes me as morally unimportant (this becomes noteworthy for the issue of experimentation, since virtually all moral and legal experimentation codes pertain to vertebrates, dubiously turning invertebrates into morally free game). But I sympathize with the general tendency within provegetarian literature to avoid fine-tuning the argument, at least in this stage of the debate. For the evidence as to animal pain (including evidence for pain in "lower" animals), see DeGrazia, *Taking Animals Seriously*, chap. 5; and Bernard E. Rollin, *The Unheeded Cry: Animal Consciousness, Animal Pain and Science* (Oxford: Oxford University Press, 1989). For a nuanced typology of morally relevant anatomical differences between animals, see Rodd, *Biology, Ethics and Animals*.

book of Genesis. The obligation to justify killing is manifested even by critics of pro-animal literature (though they of course challenge the specific cases wherein killing animals is justified). It is consensual, then, that killing animals for no good reason (even if it is painless) is wrong. Why? Proposed answers include appeals to the shared *intuition* that killing an animal is wrong (exemplified, for instance, by avoiding stepping on animals);[5] to the loss of their experiential opportunities; to the deprivation of achieving their potential; to the principle of minimizing the pain that is inevitably involved in killing; or to the opportunity of minimizing harm even when that harm does not involve pain (after defending the idea that a being can be harmed even if it cannot conceptualize the harm as present or impending). Other answers have been suggested: whatever makes us see the painless killing of people as harm cannot be restricted to humans once one attempts to clarify why the painless killing of humans is wrong. Or, killing an animal takes from it all that it has (regardless of how this affects the overall calculus of pleasure and pain, that is, whether the animal can be replaced by another experiencing animal) and it is unjust to do so when this can be avoided. Or, might cannot make right.

Such answers have been mounted from different perspectives within pro-animal literature and have been brought into conflict in the past since many provegetarian authors disagree on the specific moral basis for diet reform. Since one goal of this chapter is to show that vegetarianism need not be an outcropping from some broader considerations regarding animal ethics, we can afford to be eclectic here: unjustified killing of animals is wrong in all the senses above. It is inevitably painful, it is an act of violence, it is probably wrong in many of the senses in which killing people for no substantial reason is wrong, and it harms the animal by taking from it all that it has regardless of the pain it does or does not experience. Like other prima facie wrongs, this one too needs to be vindicated when it is done. Whether or not killing for food is a sufficient justification will be taken up later, but contesting the idea that killing animals as such harms them, as the antivegetarian claims, requires substantial arguments that can unsettle some very strong and widely shared convictions.

Critics may object to my appeals to shared beliefs. Beliefs do not turn into truths merely because they happen to be endorsed by a collective. Yet this objection ignores the distinction between justifying claims and examining what follows from these claims, assuming that they are held. Antivegetarianism clashes with beliefs most of us hold. "Too bad for these beliefs" is a possible reply, but what does it mean in this context? Deny animal pain and you are there with pre-Darwinian bioethics. Dismiss pain's moral relevance and you join company with all kinds of sadists.

---

[5] See Tardiff, "Simplifying the Case for Vegetarianism."

Peter Carruthers is admirably consistent when he claims that torturing a cat when the torturer is unseen is morally unproblematic. Swallowing this horrifying counterintuitive outcome of his own version of a direct/ indirect duties approach (rather than seeing it as a *reductio* of it) is Carruthers's own suggestion. Antivegetarians will have to endorse a strange position of this kind on pain of inconsistency. Claiming that entities are not harmed when they are painlessly killed is a sophism: if it is invalid in the case of humans, why should it persuade in the case of animals (unless "harm" is a species-dependent notion, but why should it be?[6]).

AGNOSTIC MEAT-EATING

How about agnostic meat-eaters? In the context of a philosophical debate, their kind of objection sounds lethal: no philosopher wants to sound as if her fundamental premises descended on her through divine inspiration and that their truth is secured by the aura with which they are endowed. Philosophers are in the business of justification, and so a demand for argumentative support is never inappropriate. On the other hand, how does one *argue* that, for example, pain is bad or that it harms the sufferer, or that if an entity can be made to suffer, then things matter to it? Frey, for example, denies that suffering is a sufficient condition for ascribing interests to an entity on the grounds that no one has given an argument showing that this is so. Now it may seem as clear as day that if an entity is in great pain, then it desperately wants to avoid this state. Things obviously *matter* to this entity, and in this sense, it has an *interest* in the termination of the pain. Frey does not deny the vivacity of this belief. He simply wants an argument for it.[7]

The agnostic meat-eater is in effect unfairly forcing his opponent into an area that is an embarrassing one for all moral philosophy. The dubiousness of the move consists of invoking general moral skepticism and dressing it up as a form of skepticism that is particular to animals, when in fact it is destructive to any argument within applied ethics. Under the guise of requiring argument in the limited context of the vegetarian debate, the agnostic meat-eater is demanding vegetarians to solve nothing less than the problem of basic beliefs in moral philosophy. The difficulty that the agnostic meat-eater taps is a sore spot for ethicists, relating to the argumentative weakness and fragility of moral reasoning in general. Take, for example, the belief that without some weighty justification,

[6] Some have argued that interests are linguistic, hence frustrating interests ("harm") can only be done to a human. Even if this is true, the notion of harm is broader than interference with interests (e.g., babies can be harmed even when they lack language).

[7] Frey, *Interests and Rights*, chap. 11.

inflicting suffering is wrong. This judgment is "basic" in the sense that it is constitutive of the notion of wrong: if someone denies such a judgment, he or she either altogether lacks the concept of wrong or is proposing some radical reform in ethics. But what is one to say if an argument in support of this judgment is required?

The position I find most plausible with regard to basic beliefs is sociological rather than argumentative: we are not *argued* into accepting the association between, say, unjustified inflicted suffering and wrong but are socialized into it. We wish to avoid suffering ourselves. This affects our dealings with others, making us aware of what they wish to avoid or what they perceive as harm. Philosophers typically do not object to such a developmental account and to its systematization by a theory of moral development of one type or another. But since someone can be socialized into Nazism too, philosophers would typically seek to avoid conflating the descriptive and the normative accounts of moral development. Philosophers will ask for argumentative backing for such ground-level preferences. Yet do we really have *arguments* why infliction of suffering on others requires justification? It seems that our "argument" is no more than our preference not to live in this way. Such a preference has its reasons and is thus rationally better than living in a world in which suffering can be arbitrarily inflicted. But an argument showing that A is rationally preferable to B should not be confused with an argument showing that B is wrong, which is what, in effect, the agnostic meat-eater is asking for.[8]

---

[8] A sociological explanation of this sort is philosophically disappointing, as it appears to replace argumentative justification with an explanation of genesis. Yet combing the classical ethical writings regarding basic beliefs does not yield better moves. Aristotle, Bentham, and Mill thought that some kinds of pain are bad, or that some pleasures are good, not because they provided arguments for this, but simply by virtue of these being objects of positive or negative desire (this, as Bentham recognized, does not shut the door to animals). Kant's second formulation of the categorical imperative—asking whether one wants to live in a world in which a particular practice is universalized—also appeals to basic unjustified preferences rather than to arguments. Moral philosophers do not like to admit that elaborate theories rest on conceptually basic desires or preferences. Many ethicists today lean to the Rawlsian approach to intuitions—we begin *media res*, with potentially replaceable considered judgments—and this already concedes that we have no better starting point than some conceptually primitive connections. Alternatively, one can try to resist intuitions altogether, in the manner of R. M. Hare. But even Hare does not manage to escape them. (For example, he does not explain the positive value of preference satisfaction—the basic notion of his theory—holding it to be some observable given, much like how Mill or Aristotle relate to the pursuit of happiness. But what would distinguish in an informative way between observable givens and intuitions?) To pretend that we have, or must have, a better procedure else we promote an irrational morality is superficial, since it presumes that Utilitarians, Kantians, or Contractarians have somehow solved the basic belief problem and have managed to avoid intuitions (which they did not). A complaint of this kind is also insensitive to the various sifting that goes on with relation to basic moral inputs. Sifting prevents a crude foundationalism regarding intuitions (a view that "if you are strongly for/against it, you must be right").

I specified five widely shared beliefs regarding animals: that killing them with no good reason (even when painless) is wrong; that they can experience pain; that their pain is morally relevant; that our dealings with them are morally different from our dealings with objects; and that their suffering should sometimes trump intense human pleasure. Denying these beliefs, as the antivegetarian does, is implausible. Agnostic meat-eaters ask for arguments for these beliefs before they would change their diet. The philosophically broad answer to this challenge relates to animals sharing morally relevant properties, as argued in the previous chapter. The narrower answer is that there is something basic and nonderived in repulsion felt toward someone torturing an animal. This reaction has little to do with rights that the animal does or does not have (nor do I think, incidentally, that the repulsion to someone torturing a child primarily relates to an infringement of rights). Each of the five beliefs is basic in this sense. Against the agnostic meat-eater I am claiming that asking for argumentative backing here is as plausible as asking for arguments in support of the belief that pain is (usually) bad. Agnostic meat-eating can function as a reasonable critique of vegetarianism only if it makes sense to raise the problematic nature of basic moral beliefs in any area of applied ethics and proposed moral reform.

Nonvegetarianism

If my argument so far is sound, nonvegetarianism should be the genuine position that a thoughtful opponent of moral vegetarianism should endorse. Nonvegetarians, I claimed, are those who oppose torturing animals and who would condemn euthanizing healthy animals for no reason. I claimed that these necessarily endorse the five beliefs above, and that therefore the important question between vegetarians and their opponents is not whether or not these beliefs are justified, but whether these beliefs imply that killing animals for the purpose of eating them is wrong. So after discarding the objections of antivegetarians and agnostic meat-eaters, we can finally take on this question: is killing animals for food wrong, given these shared assumptions?

Evaluating the morality of killing animals for food begins by breaking up "food" into its two components: nutrition and pleasure. Broad agreement exists as to the ability to have a fully nutritious vegetarian diet. At the same time, for most of us such a diet cannot compete with the culinary pleasure afforded by a nonvegetarian food. This clarifies the moral issue, which is no longer the moral status of killing animals *for food*, but killing animals for the unique and irreplaceable culinary pleasure that eating them affords. In his *Animal Rights and Wrongs*, Roger Scruton draws a distinction that avoids the unpleasant sound that killing for pleasure has (he is discussing angling), saying that one does not kill for fun (which connotes sadism), but killing is the price of fun.[9] Scruton's point is a good one: angling, hunting, or eating animal flesh is not sadistic. And this is why the description I choose is "killing for pleasure" rather than "killing for sadistic pleasure."

Enter pleasure. The distinct, irreplaceable, and at times intense pleasure of eating animal flesh need not be denied. Animal flesh not only opens up numerous culinary possibilities but also functions as a focus of many social and religious activities, such as the outdoor barbecue and the Christmas turkey. All such pleasures are denied to vegetarians, who instead become social spoilsports who force nonvegetarians to modify the traditional character of these. Some vegetarians will say that in their own internal hedonistic calculus, these losses are superseded by a new kind of pleasure, involving a sense of moral completeness and perhaps even purity that comes with doing the right thing.[10] Yet for other vegetarians (me) such talk is too abstract, and their moral choice is experienced as a downright loss. Personally, I am even put off by vegetarians who seem to never have had much of a zeal for eating meat, and I lose sympathy when I read passages in the writings of moral vegetarians in which "vegetarian cuisine" is praised over its immoral alternative. The unhedonistic (and therefore humanly narrow) perspective regarding the meaning of eating that sometimes animates such writings—R. M. Hare admits that he and his wife hardly eat out and so his demivegetarianism is not difficult for him—alienates vegetarians such as myself, who have had very intense experiences in eating (as well as cooking) meat, and thus experience their own moral choice as extracting a high price indeed.

Does the harm involved in killing animals trump such loss? The superficial way of framing this question is in terms of moral values as opposed to pleasures. The superficiality resides in the way by which casting the question in this way plays into the hands of the moral vegetarian. Since pursuing moral values typically involves curtailing pleasures or the pursuit of pleasures, underscoring the pleasures of eating animal flesh is simply beside the (moral) point: a case for moral vegetarianism need not be required to show that vegetarianism is the happiest or most pleasurable

[9] Scruton, *Animal Rights and Wrongs*, 3d ed. (London: Metro Books, 2000), 119.

[10] Here is, for example, Mohandas Gandhi: "And I would say that I have found from my own experience, and the experience of thousands of friends and companions, that they find satisfaction, so far as vegetarianism is concerned, from the moral basis they have chosen for sustaining vegetarianism." From "Diet and Morality," in *Ethical Vegetarianism: From Pythagoras to Peter Singer*, ed. K. S. Walters and L. Portmess (Albany: SUNY Press, 1999), 144.

way to live, but that it is the moral way to do so even if it does prescribe
tough limitations. People who justify eating animal flesh through saying
that the pleasure this gives them overrides the wrong done to animals
have, in effect, conceded the moral claims of the vegetarians.

The deeper way of framing the question is not in terms of a value-
pleasure opposition, but in terms of conflicting values. Pleasures are not
necessarily distinct from values. Some pleasures are goods, the pursuit of
which is itself a value. Culinary values need not be moral values. But they
can still constitute values (rather than pleasures) that compete with the
value of avoiding eating animal flesh. Alternatively, a person may hold
that all values (hedonic ones included) are moral, maintaining that this
stems from an overarching eudaimonistic principle that governs ones
choices and form of life. Both alternatives frame the vegetarian debate as
a clash between values rather than as a choice between what is pleasing
and what is morally correct. What is the vegetarian response to such
formulations?

Commensurating pleasures and deprivations (or balancing pleasures
against values or values against conflicting values) is notoriously difficult
to clarify theoretically. We daily make such evaluations on a private as
well as institutional level without a unified theory regarding how we do
this. When they are questioned, our preferences ultimately lack probative
force. Avoiding killing humans for fun is today a trivial judgment in
which one compares values and pleasures. Yet gladiator-fighting indicates that people did take pleasure in deadly fights. Can such pleasure of
many be trumped by the value of the lives of gladiators? Today, one
would assert that no pleasure or aggregate of pleasures of this kind justifies the death of another. Such pleasures are immoral, and the craving
that such pursuits satisfy can be replaced by nondeadly sports. Suppose,
now, that a hypothetical defender of fights to the death teleported from
some Roman arena denies that such substitutes provide the same intense
pleasure that fights to the death involve (the analogy to the vegetarian
issue being claims of the "Nothing done to tofu will compete with a juicy
steak" sort). We cannot simply demand that he give up his pleasure, if he
challenges us to explain why the death involved in the practices he loves
so much overrides his intense pleasure. We can appeal to notions like
rights or the sanctity of life. But these make no sense in the nonegalitar-
ian setting of ancient Rome and must strike him as dubious and forced
innovations. His judgments will probably resemble those who today reject the applications of notions like rights to animals. The debate would
probably stop there.

Comparative judgments regarding conflicting values or goods lack
probative force. They spring from a rich matrix of sensitivities that do
not exist universally. Rejecting the moral status of gladiator-fighting

from our present perspective is much easier than doing so from within a cultural outlook that has not yet devised an egalitarian conception and a sensitivity to the importance of human life. But this is a practical difference. On the level of rational debate the impasse is as fierce. What can one *say* to a defender of fights to the death? What constitutes a good argument showing that the pleasure of such sports cannot outweigh the harm they involve? We reach foundational issues in ethics: the probative status of evaluations; their convention-related status versus a possible transconvention implicit structure from which they emerge; whether persuading a radical dissenter is in fact a plausible test for a moral position; what constitutes proof in ethics; the possible justification for reforming present practices and sentiments.

I will not plunge into these. Analogous past cases in which curtailing benefits and pleasures from one group of entities because such involves overwhelming harm to another group did not proceed from discovering a solution to the foundational problems of ethics. Egalitarian social movements succeed primarily due to numerous pragmatic contingencies. Their moral case is substantiated through tapping sentiments that sometimes need to be created, until the claims they make turn from idiosyncratic preaching into vivid and action-guiding prescriptions. Vegetarianism is in the same boat as pre-nineteenth-century feminism or early-eighteenth-century abolitionism: the sentiments that are capable of transforming the preferences within the privileged group so that the harm done will be perceived as overwhelming in relation to the benefits gained are nonexistent or weak.

The upshot of all this is that one cannot *prove* that killing animals for the pleasure involved in eating them is wrong. One can show that killing versus pleasure is the actual equation, and that each instance of eating animal flesh is one application of this equation with reference to a particular animal's death and a particular pleasure. One can then point to the continuity between vegetarianism and other social causes that we typically regard as encapsulating and promoting moral progress, in which overwhelming harm requires limiting pleasures.[11]

---

[11] It is many times noted that pro-animal literature appeals to similarities between liberating animals and egalitarian social movements. Early writings in the modern version of the pro-animal movement in the 1970s have done much to press the analogy here (Ryder and Singer on speciesism are the best examples). Note that the argument over this analogy has several layers: first, an egalitarian outlook has little to do with the empirical fact of an actual equality in capacity between the privileged and nonprivileged classes. Second, systematic bias against a class of entities usually depends on erroneously regarding a difference between the entities to have moral significance. Third (the point I am making above), a concern for morality or fairness in these cases always carries a price, a curtailing of certain pleasures within the privileged class. For a detailed defense of the idea that reforming animal-related practices cannot and need not be proved but rather is to be predicated on

PERSONAL ACTION AND GENERAL OUTCOME

Yet since personally refraining from eating animal flesh will not save a single animal, endorsing personal vegetarianism does not follow from recognition of the immorality of killing animals for food, or from upholding the desirability of collective vegetarianism. Provegetarians bridge this gap either by arguing that personal action may affect large-scale outcome (the analogy being voting: negligible impact is overwhelmingly likely; yet overwhelming impact is a possibility that calls for personal action), or by arguing that consuming products that are made through immoral actions exemplifies the wrong kind of virtue (obtuseness, callousness, cruelty), or by emphasizing symbolic support and symbolic protest.[12]

Opponents of vegetarianism will avoid formulating this problem as a critique of vegetarianism since if one accepts the "Voter's Paradox" reasoning here—a reasoning according to which the benefits of a large-scale desired action are causally detached from personal action—one is opening a Pandora's box. Tax paying, cooperating with a draft, personal charitable aid to large-scale goals that one endorses, will all become irrational. The challenge for vegetarian theory is here not one of responding to a viable critique, but of clarifying the connection between consumption and killing when one's own actions cannot modify outcome for future animals.[13]

General connections between personal action and promoting a desirable goal are one type of account that comes to mind. Eddy Zemach, a moral vegetarian, tells me that for him, fairness is the notion doing the work here (reducing the killing of animals is one's objective, and doing one's fair share in promoting this goal prescribes avoiding eating flesh). Zemach is partly right: such appeal to fairness is a conceptual link that operates in numerous cases in which the personal and the collective are linked. But I think that we can get closer to the particularities that distinguish the vegetarian example. Avoiding eating flesh, if one believes that it is collectively wrong, is not merely a case of doing one's fair share. Nor is the problem merely one of flawed integrity.[14]

---

such reform being continuous with other moral concerns, such as fairness, minimizing suffering, and developing a better character, see Sapontzis, *Morals, Reason, and Animals.*

[12] Nathan Nobis surveys these routes in his "Vegetarianism and Virtue: Does Consequentialism Demand Too Little?" *Social Theory and Practice* 28 (1) (2002): 135–56.

[13] Some vegetarians believe that their diet personally diminishes the amount of animals killed. While I regard this as erroneous wishful thinking, the following argument on a deeper connection between consumption and killing is consistent with holding that the vegetarian is also personally affecting animal welfare.

[14] Daniel Statman suggested to me that integrity and avoiding hypocrisy may be the important aspects here.

The most promising route to get at the specific moral structure linking the killing of animals and the consumption of meat is Curnutt's attempts to relate to the killing and the consumption as two parts of the same wrong.[15] Curnutt defends this idea through the principle that it is wrong to cooperate and benefit from a defeat of the basic well-being of others. This principle explains the wrongness of consumption by tying it with the harm done to the animal.

But the bond is actually tighter than benefiting or cooperating. It surfaces when focusing on the philosophy of action implied by Curnutt's "two parts of the same wrong." Unfortunately, provegetarian literature has here relied on misleading analogies between eating animals and using human remains that have been transformed into objects (favorite examples are using soap or lamps made out of the remains of Jewish victims of the Nazis, or finding and wearing a ring made of human bone). Instrumental usage of human body parts is a symbolic demeaning of a person after death. Jews were not killed to produce soap. Using such "objects" is wrong since it participates in demeaning a person. Such horrid examples also involve disgust, the moral status of which is complex: disgust is itself an amoral psychological fact that carries moral implications.[16] Killing animals for food is different. Pleasure rather than repulsion is experienced. Another difference is that animals are also not perceived as being demeaned by using them for the purpose of producing food, clothing, or footwear.

Better analogies that get us to the operating ethical depth-structure of moral vegetarianism are watching snuff movies, or enjoying art that involves body parts (Melanesian head decoration). Victims of snuff movies (I will assume that such movies exist) have been killed so that someone

---

[15] Jordan Curnutt, "A New Argument for Vegetarianism," *Journal of Social Philosophy* 28 (1997): 153–72. Tom Regan speaks of meat eaters being "causally implicated" in a wrong but does not discuss the special nature of the causal link in his "The Moral Basis of Vegetarianism," in *All That Dwells Within* (Berkeley: University of California Press, 1982), 1–39.

[16] This last point is indicated by Herodotus in the *History of the Persian Wars*: a discovered society repelled by the idea of burial, favoring instead the eating of the dead as a mark of respect for them. I see nothing immoral in changed cultural norms in which human remains are used in various ways, soap production included. Indeed, commodification of one's future corpse can be a good way to promote highly important goals, like enlarging the available reservoirs of organs for transplanting, thus greatly decreasing present suffering and death of living people. Some uses that can be imagined are disturbing or repulsive, and given such responses they are then immoral; but the responses themselves rest on amoral conventions. We are attached to our bodies, and we care about what happens to them after we die. This is a fact about present human psychology, and it has moral implications. But should we come to see this care as an irrational sentiment, there is nothing immoral about using bodies in ways that are less appealing than as organ reservoirs.

would watch them die later. Here the consumption is a *completion* of the initial action. By "completion" I refer to a temporally extended action, in which the part of the action done in the past anticipated and was predicated on an unspecified individual who will function in a designated way. By filling that abstract individual's projected position, one makes concrete and completes the action.[17] The snuff movie victim was not just killed; she was killed *so that someone* would watch her die later (analogously: the animal was not simply killed; it was killed *so it would be* worn or eaten later). These actions have an extended temporal structure: a specified beginning with particular agents and victims, and a specified yet unpopulated end. One completes this disembodied structure when becoming *that* undesignated agent.

Apart from completing a temporally extended wrong through consumption, there is, too, the conceptually distinct wrong of participating in a wrong practice, even when one's consumption does not increase suffering. Wearing rings made of human bones is an appropriate example here, though in our context it conflates several distinct kinds of harm, some of which do not apply in the animal case, so I shall avoid it. A better example is paying for services provided by child-prostitution establishments that exist in some countries. Doing so does not necessarily intensify the pain or harm done to the children involved. The potential "customer" would only be one more indistinguishable client in the long day of the child being prostituted. One can even make a difference for the better: say, tipping generously or behaving nicer than other clients would. Morally avoiding such practices involves the sort of denied participation I am outlining, rather than assumptions regarding consequential change brought about through one's actions.

MORAL VEGETARIANISM

Moral vegetarianism, then, is the position according to which animals should not be killed for food when nutritional alternatives are available. To eat animals is to participate in and to complete a morally wrong act. The emphasis is on refraining from participation in a wrong done to an entity, where one's participation is not necessarily an intensification of the harm being done, but an endorsement of a wrong practice. This understanding of vegetarianism avoids causal connections between vegetarianism and a reduction achieved or envisaged in the number of animals

---

[17] Another way of articulating this thought, suggested to me by Stan Godlovitch, is that by consumption one is in effect commissioning the killing. This formulation has an air of backward causality that I mean to avoid above.

raised or killed for food. Nor does it assume that private vegetarianism will lead to collective vegetarianism, or that vegetarianism is a causally effective type of protest against the wrongs of factory-farming, as is assumed, for example, by demivegetarians (people who do not see anything wrong in killing animals for food but are appalled by factory-farming and so eat small quantities of meat, thus protesting against current farming methods).

Note that no equality is assumed between the value or sufferings of animals and of humans. This brand of moral vegetarianism does not require a prior assumption that speciesism is wrong or a belief in animal rights. In addition, this formulation of vegetarianism allows for eating and using animals that have not died from planned killing for the purpose of eating them. Some vegetarians will disagree with this conclusion (e.g., Cora Diamond in her "Eating Meat and Eating People"). This position also says nothing against raising animals for food. While the vegetarianism I defend will avoid participating in current factory-farming practices as well, the position does not prescribe a ban on raising animals for the purpose of eating them after they die on their own. While there are excellent culinary and prudential reasons to refrain from what Sapontzis calls "scavenging," I do not see a moral reason to do so. A more inviting possibility is using fur or leather products that come from animals that have died on their own. There are no prudential reasons to avoid this, and no moral reasons to do so either.

Vegetarianism thus construed does not entail veganism. The question of the morality of *any* use of animals for food products differs from use that involves killing them for the purpose of eating them. While many uses of animals are wrong, unlike killing them, the very use of animals for eggs and dairy is not wrong as such. Using animals for these is consistent with their welfare, in the sense that they can lead comfortable and painless lives. Here commodification can actually work for animals rather than against them, since it generates a financial incentive to preserve them.[18] Since modern factory-farming techniques for obtaining dairy and eggs are extremely cruel, participating in such practices is wrong too. But such a ban on participation is different. First, this ban prescribes selective consumption, which still allows for consumption of egg and dairy products that are raised in morally acceptable ways. Second, avoiding egg and dairy because of the immoral production practices these rely on cannot be conceptualized in terms of avoiding the completion of or participation in a wrong in the same sense of the prostituted

---

[18] On commodifying animals as a benefit to them, see R. A. Posner, "Animal Rights: Legal, Philosophical, and Pragmatic Perspectives," in *Animal Rights: Current Debates and New Directions*, ed. Martha C. Nussbaum and Cass R. Sunstein (Oxford: Oxford University Press, 2004), 51–77.

child or the killed animals example. Unlike eggs or milk, no reform done to a child-prostitution establishment will justify participation. More needs to be said here, but I postpone doing so because the vegan-vegetarian issue will be taken up in detail in chapter 6.

"BUT EATING ANIMALS IS IN THEIR INTEREST"

Leahy, Scruton, and Hare have argued that collective vegetarianism involves the inexistence of billions of potential animals and the possible extinction of species that would not exist if there was no financial incentive to breed them.[19] This argument is often used in conversation; the attempt being to embarrass the vegetarian into admitting that the opponent's eating practices are a positive good to the killed animals, thus reversing the moral poles of the debate. If collective vegetarianism is bad for animals, then personal vegetarianism predicated on the immorality of killing for eating (rather than only a protest against modalities of rearing) is counterproductive from the standpoint of animals. Call this the "eating-animals-benefits-them" argument, or EABT for short. Here is Hare's version of EABT:

> From the point of view of such a [roughly utilitarian] theory it would seem that the issue about *killing* animals, as distinct from causing them suffering, resolves itself into, not the question of whether it is all right to kill animals, but the question of how many lives animals, of different species including the human, we ought to cause there to be. . . . What we ought to be doing is to maximize the amount of quality-adjusted life years . . . of sentient beings. And I do not believe that we should be doing this if we refrained from eating animals. The reason is that if we gave up eating animals the market for meat would vanish, and no more animals would be raised for meat-production. . . . This thought gives me pause when I walk in the fields around my home in England and see a great many apparently happy animals, all destined to be eventually eaten. . . . In our village there is also a trout farm. The fish start their lives in moderately commodious ponds and have what I guess is a pleasant life for fish, with plenty to eat. In due course they are lifted out in buckets and put immediately into tanks in the farm buildings. Purchasers select their fish, which is then killed by being banged smartly on the head

---

[19] M.P.T. Leahy, *Against Liberation: Putting Animals in Perspective* (London and New York: Routledge, 1991), 210; R. M. Hare, "Why I Am Only a Demi-Vegetarian," in *Essays on Bioethics* (Oxford: Clarendon Press, 1993), 219–36; Scruton, *Animal Rights and Wrongs*.

and handed to the customer. I am fairly certain that, if given the choice, I would prefer the life, all told, of such a fish to that of almost any fish in the wild, and to non-existence.[20]

Hare is actually running together two distinct questions: the first involves the benefits of being raised for food from the standpoint of the animal in comparison to nonexistence (conceived both from the perspective of the individual animal destined for slaughter and from the projected perspective of entire species that would not exist if this did not further some human interest). The second relates to killing by human hand, a process that can be better for the animal than "natural" death.

Let us begin with being killed by humans (as opposed to being brought into existence by humans and then killed by them). This argument is sometimes made with regard to hunting: it is said that the hunted animal is better off being killed by hunters or their dogs than experiencing the kinds of death that await it in the wild. This version of EABT is a pretense. Hare is not saying that killing the trout is a benefit for it *now*. Being banged "smartly" is obviously not in the interest of the trout (we are to think that Hare is imagining a healthy trout, not one that is in pain, or dying through other harsh means, or about to be eaten by a larger fish). An already existing animal has an obvious interest in prolonging its life, assuming it is healthy and not suffering from some other cause. Killing cannot be a benefit for it. So the killing itself is rarely a boon, and when one presents a case for a killing that benefits the animal, one reaches criteria resembling those of euthanized companion animals that are mostly killed for their own good. In fact, since humans are highly successful voluntary predators—"voluntary" in the sense that they do not have to hunt foxes or fish—we can imagine these creatures relieved to hear that such hunting is eliminated, and that they have so many less predators to worry about (recall that EABT asks us to hypothesize regarding what benefits animals).

But Hare's argument with regard to the fish is somewhat different: being raised and killed for human consumption makes for an *overall better life* for the trout than being a fish in the wild, or simply a nonexistent fish. This is the more popular version of EABT. Against this, one can obviously challenge the plausibility of arguing from the relative good of

---

[20] Hare, "Why I Am Only a Demi-Vegetarian," 227–28. Pro-animal literature did not fail to mention the structural similarity of such claims to past justifications of slavery: "[The abolition of slavery] would be extreme cruelty to the African savages, a portion of whom it saves from massacre, or intolerable bondage in their own country, and introduces into a much happier state of life." Citation ascribed to James Boswell and is given in M. Spiegel, *The Dreaded Comparison: Human and Animal Slavery* (New York: Mirror Books, 1996), 73.

nonexistent entities. But I shall avoid this line and assume that it makes sense to say that an entity benefits from being brought into existence. Vegetarians deal with this argument through analogous thought-experiments with regard to potential humans that will be victimized through practices that would, at the same time, bring them into existence. We would have no problem judging immoral a pedophilic society that brings some children into the world in order to sexually exploit them—providing them with otherwise pleasant living conditions—and then killing them painlessly when they mature and lose their sexual appeal, justifying the exploitation and killing through the benefits of being born; banning a reform on the pretense that it would prescribe nonexistence to these children. Or consider human cloning for the purpose of creating people who live pleasant and short lives, functioning as organ banks that would not exist without this purpose. If these analogies are valid then EABT is wrong. These practices cannot be vindicated through appealing to the benefits of creating the victims, when one pretends to do so from the victim's own standpoint.

Advocates of EABT will either drop EABT as a plausible justification or argue that there is some important disanalogy between human and nonhuman animals: human life is endowed with a different kind of value. They will argue that the considerations that could support killing people are different from those befitting animals, which is why the justification does not carry over from nonhuman to human animals. Perhaps this is what is meant by the attribution of "sanctity" to human life: that the value of human life is noninstrumental, it does not reside in life being merely a means for opportunities, experiences, or actualizing one's potential, but in some intrinsic dignity that human life possesses. And so the defender of EABT appears to hold that the value of human life not only is distinct, but also overrides these other ends in the sense that some very positive experiences and some worthy actualization of one's potential will not justify existence as such. The defender of EABT will then go on to say that animals' lives are different. They are not sacred, they lack the dignity we perceive in human lives, and they do have mere instrumental value. Note, though, that all this leads the defender of EABT to a strange result: the inferior and instrumental value of animal life gets potential animals some benefits over less fortunate potential human animals. Animals get to exist, flourish, and die, whereas potential humans are so valuable that they cannot exist at all.

This outcome is surprising, but one can still swallow it. Being special has its limitations, and not existing, even when such existence is in one's interest, is one of them. But the surprising result calls for thoughts about the valuation of life that lead to it. The thought-experiments above could be construed in ways that turn the lives of potential exploited children or cloned organ donors into partly pleasant ones. Since such practices do benefit their potential victims, explicating what is morally wrong with them relates to the ambivalence of "worth": short of extreme scenarios, most lives are worth living from the perspective of the potential beings who live them (since some positive experiential value overrides no value). At the same time, life's value is not determined solely through this internal perspective. Virtually all lives are *worth* living, yet, some lives *should not* be lived. This dual evaluation of life's value is not restricted to human lives. No one holds that it is justified to bring animals to the world in order to torture them to death after they lead several years of pleasant living. Raising animals for food need not be similar to torturing them. But the torture analogy shows that it is insufficient to point out the prudential benefit a practice has for the purpose of its evaluation, since such evaluation involves a second, *qualitative* component that EABT leaves out. Apart from the quantitative and qualitative dimensions (that is, whether a life is or is not lived and its quality), there is also what may be called a "teleological" dimension: some qualitatively reasonable lives should not be lived since some ends for lives that are lived morally pervert or present a misrecognition regarding what having a life means (the case of the euthanized puppies exemplifies this, or consider leading a pleasant but radically illusory life from beginning to end—a *Matrix* scenario). When the triple aspect of life's evaluation is recognized, it is no longer sufficient to point out the benefit of living from the standpoint of the animal. One also has to factor in qualitative and teleological dimensions of such lives. This undermines the EABT argument that rests on prudential considerations alone.

The problems of employing EABT do not end there. EABT also prescribes a too conservative stance with regard to factory-farming, a stance that Hare and Scruton would not like to adopt since both wish to see factory-farms reformed. By reducing to a minimum the price of raising animals and thus making meat cheaper and affordable for many consumers, factory-farms enable many more animals to exist than the number of animals raised through traditional farming methods. Stop factory-farming by substantially reforming quality of life for farm animals, and you inevitably diminish the number of existing animals, probably by millions. Factory-farming prescribes harsh lives for animals, though—defenders of factory-farming will point out—it is better than, say, a life of nonstop torture and arguably better than not existing at all. An obtuse owner of a factory-farm would deploy EABT not merely to vindicate eating meat, but also to prevent qualitative reform involving reduction of animal suffering. She would claim that any such reduction in suffering would inevitably reduce many lives of potential animals (consider, for example, the financial implications of requiring that laying hens have more room to move around in large-scale poultry farming). If eating animals benefits them, then raising them in the most financially efficient way is in their favor too. It is even possible that the quality of living in such factories should be *reduced* further, thus enabling even more animals to exist (preventing any movement at all for chickens rather then just limiting their movement severely may enable such factories to double or triple the amount of living chickens). No philosopher who has taken the trouble to examine the particularities of factory-farming accepts this conclusion.[21]

Aside from this, EABT also has an interesting flip side: if killing animals for food and eating them is truly held to be a benefit to these animals (because such practice brings them into existence), the inverse holds too: animals that can thrive without humans breeding them—say, fish— should not be eaten since, obviously, such killing has nothing to do with their benefit. The same holds for cows and hens, which would still exist in large numbers even if they were not killed for food, as the incentive to raise them for eggs and milk would preserve them in large numbers. And so this objection to vegetarianism actually goes some way in furthering the aims of moral vegetarians.

Is Collective Vegetarianism Desirable for Animals?

EABT aside, we are still obliged to face the question of the desirability of a vegetarian utopia from the standpoint of animals. Suppose that farm-animal husbandry is reformed, that factory-farming is abolished, and that animals are only killed for their own benefit or when they endanger people. Suppose that laying hens are still raised for eggs, cows for milk, and all such animals live in uncrowded farms that are encouraged to invest in raising these animals for these products. Such animals are killed only when they are old, wounded, or ill. In some cases they are then eaten or sold as food; their bodies are used for the production of numerous products like leather or pet food. There is nothing so far immoral in such a world. But what prospects does such a world hold for bulls, male chicks, or hogs in general, which have no such "goods" to deliver and are today not raised at all (in the case of virtually all male chicks, which are killed upon birth) or are raised only for their flesh (as are calves and pigs)?

Presenting a vegetarian ideal is a theoretical challenge, not a practical one. The question is whether vegetarian theory is flawed since it is

[21] Hare, it is true, is speaking of "quality-adjusted life years," not simply of existence. But the obtuse farmer I am imagining will say that a hen's life in a crowded cage is better than no life, and since Hare is not explicating how negative quality is to be weighed against the benefits of existence, it is not clear how endorsers of Hare's position can respond.

predicated on an ideal that is detrimental for some farm animals (there might come a time when the question becomes a practical one, but for us the question is merely theoretical). Is collective vegetarianism bad for some animals? One possible answer is that if the choice is between exploiting some animals and the nonexistence of these animals, a moral world should opt for the latter. According to this answer, a vegetarian ideal world will not include any of these animals: the cow, the pig, and the hen will follow the dodo. But milder solutions are possible. Selective artificial insemination can solve some problems—at least for poultry and cattle—by the time that collective vegetarianism will pose a real "threat," should that time ever come. Artificial insemination is widely practiced today with regard to cattle and turkeys, and more recently has been made possible in chickens. Semen differentiation as part of these practices is not technologically inconceivable (it exists for humans) and would solve the moral problems involved in the birth of "unproductive" males while preserving the species. Short of this, vegetarian legislation, should that ever happen, can make the killing of "nonproductive" animals illegal and require that the cost of raising them along with their "more productive" sisters be shared by the consumers of eggs, milk, leather, and wool. Indeed, such "compensation" to these animals—conceived of as kinds rather than individuals—can morally justify the use to which they are put and answer the moral misgivings of vegans: without eggs, milk, and posthumous use of their bodies, these animals along with their many brothers (in the case of chickens, more than half of chicks are "useless" males) would not exist at all.

The vegetarian utopia's real problem (and, I must admit, somewhat ironic in the case of a book written by a Jew) is with pigs. Negative ecological consequences of setting some pigs free at various places on the planet and letting them have their opportunity to survive as a wild species may outweigh the envisaged benefits, even if this option is at all feasible. Keeping the species alive through confining some of them in zoos is a solution only under the assumption that zoos themselves are morally justified institutions. Recent literature toys with the idea of "positive obligations" or "negative responsibility" to animals, the idea being a duty to benefit animals rather than focusing exclusively on the obligation not to harm them.[22] Such ideas may be based on an obligation to save an endangered species, especially one that, like pigs, has been heavily exploited. Of course, conceiving of such degrees of charitable behavior in a world where human lives, misery, illness, and poverty are routinely ignored is a fantasy. Again, the issue is theoretical, not practical. Pigs present the same moral problem as do lab mice that remain healthy after

[22] DeGrazia, *Taking Animals Seriously*, 272–78; Nussbaum, *Frontiers of Justice*, 372–80.

they have been experimented upon and are today killed by the millions since they cannot be reused in further experimentation. One cannot ask scientists to set these free in "the wild." Yet we can probably do better than gas healthy mice in carbon dioxide tanks, as is routinely done now.

Collective vegetarianism will not involve extinction of species that are exploited today. The cow, chicken, and pig will exist. The reduction in number in some of these species would only correct the artificial growth in the number of lives that should not be lived and are lived now.

Chapter 4

KILLING FOR KNOWLEDGE

WIDE AGREEMENT EXISTS that experimenting on animals[1] in ways that harm or kill them is permissible but is to be limited: few hold that minute advancements in knowledge justify any degree of animal suffering and death.[2] The concern for limitation registers a deeper tension that underlies the moral status of research: if animals suffer, if killing animals is on a different moral footing from modifying objects, what justifies killing them and causing them pain in order to advance knowledge, test and devise medical and nonmedical products, or determine their toxicity levels? What allows us to kill them in classroom demonstrations?

When we say that the interest to advance knowledge or promote product safety for humans trumps the pain and death of animals, we are assuming that human ends are more important than animal welfare.[3] This

---

[1] To reiterate, throughout this discussion the term "animals" will cover both "high" and "low" nonhuman animals that are experimented upon. Species-specific arguments that relate only to "higher" species that have much in common with humans (e.g., Wise, *Rattling the Cage*) will not be discussed. I fail to see the moral significance of the distinction between vertebrates and invertebrates (legal restrictions on animal-based experiments are usually confined to the former), since being a vertebrate or an invertebrate does not overlap with pain and suffering in any clear way. For all we know, rudimentary nervous systems may even create and conduct more intense pain than the more complex ones.

[2] Moral restrictions on research are usually called the "three R's" (reduction, refinement, replacement—terms introduced in 1959 by Russell and Burch's *The Principles of Humane Experimental Technique*). Typically, researchers are required to (1) have the experiment's objective reviewed in advance, preferably by bodies external to the research institution (where such examination consists of a cost-benefit assessment regarding the need to use animals relative to the experiment's importance and anticipated success); (2) use the most "inferior" animals; (3) minimize the number of animals used; (4) give analgesia when it does not interfere with the experiment's objectives; (5) practice euthanasia; and (6) have named individuals responsible for pre- and postoperative animal welfare.

[3] The precise nature of such importance can mean various things. As mentioned earlier, B. A. Brody, in "Defending Animal Research," has profitably distinguished between the "lexical priority" of human over nonhuman interests (which he associates with U.S. animal-experimentation legislation) and "discounting of interests" (which he associates with European legislation). "Lexical priority" means that any human interest overrides any animal interest; "discounting" means that some highly important animal interest can override an unimportant human interest. Both "lexical" and "discounting" approaches are opposed to the equal consideration of interests, which Brody attributes to animal advocates. The idea of "equal consideration of interests" is itself debatable within pro-animal philosophers. DeGrazia (*Taking Animals Seriously*, 63) has added a further distinction between

assumption is left untouched even in the most pro-animal legislation. Countries such as the United Kingdom, Norway, the Netherlands, or Sweden, which have introduced the most progressive and ambitious legislation, still perceive experiments as morally justified (Nazi Germany being a glaring and disturbing counterexample).[4] In this chapter, I do not attack the assumption that humans are more valuable than nonhuman animals—"valuable" either simply due to species membership or because their interests, pleasures, capabilities, and so on count for more—but undermine its capacity to function as a plausible vindication of research. Much antiresearch philosophical literature is devoted to challenging the discounting of animal interests. This chapter examines whether or not animal-based research is morally credible if one grants the superiority of humans. I will argue that a speciesist outlook does not morally validate research.

ARGUMENTATIVE STRATEGY

Four distinct operations are at play when the assumption that humans are more valuable than animals serves as a springboard to a justification of research. These are sometimes run together, diffusing into each other, so avoiding confusion requires demarcating and discussing them separately. First, people value the capacities in which humans excel more than the capacities of animals. Animal-based experimentation is excused given the necessity to harm either humans or animals and the inferiority of the latter. Second, care for human suffering overrides sympathy for animals. Third, humans possess an entirely different level of moral standing than animals. Since humans deserve more, saving a single human life justifies sacrificing many animals. Fourth, terminating experimentation will harm humans. The damage will be in the form of either life-saving

---

equal consideration and equal treatment, claiming that the former need not imply the latter. These finer distinctions regarding the meaning of "overriding" and "equality" will not concern the following argument (though DeGrazia's distinction can be read as anticipating some of my argument in [3] below).

   [4] The ban on animal-based experiments in Nazi Germany extended only to some districts. The British and Dutch systems includes a tripartite division of severity of animal suffering—"mild," "moderate," and "substantial"—that is used to approve or prevent experiments that are evaluated according to their relative importance: trivial experimental goals cannot validate inflicting "substantial" pain. For a comparative analysis of legislative practices (which may be somewhat dated), see K. Dolan, *Ethics, Animals and Science* (Oxford: Blackwell Science, 1999), chap. 13; J. Hampson (1987) "Legislation: A Practical Solution to the Vivisection Dilemma?" in *Vivisection in Historical Perspective*, ed. N. A. Rupke (London: Croom Helm, 1987), 314–39; R. Preece and L. Chamberlain, *Animal Welfare and Human Values* (Waterloo, Ont.: Wilfried Laurier University Press, 1995 [1993]), chap. 6.

products that will not be devised, or risk to human subjects of experimental drugs that have not been sifted through in vivo experiments. These, then, are four different formulations of the idea that humans have greater value than animals and that, accordingly, it is morally permissible to experiment on them: we *ascribe greater importance* to what humans are, we *care* more for them, we think that they *deserve* more, and we think that by experimenting on animals, we *minimize the harm* done to humans.

Challenging these four claims is possible, but I will avoid this. I shall also assume that these assumptions are *justified*, not merely widely shared. Instead, I plan to ask whether they exonerate the killing animals as part of research. If they fail to provide such support, we lose the commonest kind of moral defense for research. We will then have to stop animal-dependent research altogether, devise a new moral defense for it, or continue it while acknowledging its immorality.

LEGITIMIZING THE QUESTION

Before examining the moral status of research, we need to ask whether such exploration is plausible given that we routinely kill huge amounts of animals for much lighter reasons. If society does not outlaw eating meat, hunting, or fishing, then, a fortiori, it cannot interfere with research that sacrifices animals for weightier reasons. This point is routinely made in proresearch propaganda, which typically compares the death toll in the meat industry or processes of "pest" control with the numbers of animals killed by experiments. One such estimate, conducted by the Research Defense Society, shows that in 1991, 11.5 animals per person were killed for food in the UK, whereas 0.05 animals per person were used (not necessarily killed) in research. The number of rodents exterminated as pests each year on average is almost four times the number of rodents killed during experiments.[5] Another way to put the same point is to say, with Webster, that an average human omnivore eats in a lifetime around seven hundred animals (not counting fish). In comparison, only four lab animals per one human life are killed (in the UK). Webster concludes that "this is not, perhaps, much to ask of Brother Mouse."[6] Picking on researchers when routine killing takes place is insincere and dubious.

[5] See Dolan, *Ethics, Animals and Science*, 170.

[6] J. Webster, *Animal Welfare: A Cool Eye Towards Eden* (Oxford: Blackwell Science, 1995), 228. He adds: "Anyone who can justify rearing and killing animals for food cannot reject the principle that it is, at the very least, equally acceptable to rear and kill animals in similar ways to improve understanding or reduce the ravages of disease."

The problem with this claim is the assumption that existing norms regarding meat eating and pest control are morally justified. True, *if* killing animals for food is justified, then, a fortiori, killing them to test product safety or devise better medication cannot be immoral. Yet it is far from clear that killing for food is morally admissible. Presented as a moral vindication of research, pointing out widespread misuses of animals for trivial reasons is plainly inadequate (the strategic dimensions of this fact do, however, compromise the practical implications of the following moral analysis, an issue to which I shall return at the end of this chapter).

At the same time, *if* eating or hunting animals is impermissible, this does not entail that research is immoral. Apart from the involvement of a weightier human interest, a major moral difference between the two kinds of killing relates to alternatives. Dieticians hold that a non-meat-based diet is nutritious, and today's supermarkets make it easily available. On the other hand, the provivisection claim is that in spite of developed alternatives, there are still no real replacements for lab animals. If this is correct, dietary reform is distinct from the moral status of vivisection in two ways: first, the latter may present a trumping human interest whereas the former does not. Second, unlike dietary reform, the established view within the scientific community regarding experimenting with animals perceives the sacrificing of animals as having no satisfactory alternatives. Both reasons make it possible to hold that killing animals for food or sport is wrong, but killing them for applied or non-applied knowledge is not. Vivisection is an autonomous issue within animal welfare.

I will now examine each of the four components of the common justification for research.

The Greater Value of Humans

Provivisection literature is specked with assertions of human superiority that are perceived as adequate support for animal experiments:

> We are a species unique in our cognitive abilities: to use just a few examples, we create beautiful sculptures, write on philosophical issues, and devise just laws. These laws, as well as tradition handed down from long ago, bind us together in a moral community. Yet, we are autonomous beings living in that community. Only we, of all species on Earth, can be held accountable for our deeds, judged guilty in a court of law. We are burdened in a way that no other species is, even to the extent of caring for other species. These

responsibilities make us special in my view and warrant special consideration and compassion. I think it follows that we owe it to our fellow man to alleviate the pain and misery of disease through biomedical research.[7]

It will obviously not do to merely assert the importance, worthiness, or cognitive advantages of humans over nonhumans as a justification of animal-based experimentation.[8] As maintained in chapter 1, establishing such superiority is disconnected from the justification of causing suffering. In what way does the superiority of A over B justify A in *doing* anything with regard to B? As antivivisectionists were always quick to point out, a race of aliens of superior cognitive and technical power is not justified in experimenting on us. A crude assertion of superiority cannot then suffice.

I am postponing to a later section the discussion of the claim that *because* humans are worthier they *deserve* more, a move that sometimes does the tacit work here, and am instead focusing on what follows from superiority as such. A subtler version of the superiority claim is that humans are not simply cognitively worthier but, unlike animals, have crossed a threshold that makes them eligible for moral consideration. Morrison can perhaps be asserting precisely that in the citation above, but there are clearer statements of this view:

> Secular moral philosophy is constructed from the perspective of moral agents who are rational stakeholders in moral controversies, and it is these stakeholders who have the dignity of being the cardinal arbiters of morality. This grants a plausible but not conclusive priority to human concerns, interests, and projects over and against considerations of the pains, pleasures, and lives of animals. It is humans who incarnate the fullness of the moral life, suggesting that the health, quality, and extension of human life should have priority

---

[7] A. R. Morrison, "Ethical Principles: Guiding the Use of Animals in Research," *The American Biology Teacher*, 65 (2) (February 2003): 106.

[8] See chapter 1 for various renderings of speciesism. In fact, to unpack the "greater value" of human life in secular terms is not easy. See S. F. Sapontzis, "On Justifying the Exploitation of Animals in Research," *Journal of Medicine and Philosophy* 13 (1988): 177–96. When this superior value mobilizes a justification of vivisection, it has repugnant consequences. This is the gist of R. G. Frey, "Vivisection, Morals and Medicine," *Journal of Medical Ethics* 9 (2) (1983): 94–97. Frey argues that explicating the greater value of human over nonhuman life in terms of richness of experience leads to the unwelcomed outcome that human lives of poor quality may be subject to experiments (given that considerations of relative quality of life justify experimenting on an entity). Sapontzis has formulated an analogous argument to the one I shall present, according to which neither utilitarianism nor Kantianism can justify the assumption that beings of superior value are entitled to exploit inferior beings.

over concerns regarding animal life. From this it follows that it is good to use animals to advantage human well-being.[9]

According to this defense of animal-based research, a disanalogy exists between the alien-human case and the human-animal one, and a sophism is involved in conceptualizing the apology for research in terms of an unjustified move from superiority to conduct. Experimenting on animals is permissible because it involves acting in relation to beings that have no moral status (or have a merely derivative moral status). This is the essence of Carl Cohen's argument:

> Humans are of such a kind that they may be the subject of experiments only with their voluntary consent. The choices they make freely must be respected. Animals are of such a kind that it is impossible for them, in principle, to give or withhold voluntary consent or to make a moral choice. What humans retain when disabled, animals have never had.[10]

Yet since categorically ostracizing animals from moral concern is implausible—as such a view cannot account for the widely shared concern to eliminate cruelty to animals or the wish to reduce their suffering—the superiority claim will in effect be quantitative: the threshold that humans pass does not mean that animals are excluded from any degree of consideration, but that animals are not entitled to a level of consideration that makes it immoral to experiment on them.

Suppose that believing in degrees of moral considerability is defensible.[11] The viability of the superiority argument would now largely depend on what "degrees" and "value" should mean. Take the second chapter's unpacking of "status" into moral protection. According to such explication, ascribing a "higher" moral status to humans would mean that humans are covered by a broader and more inclusive range of moral entitlements and protections relative to nonhuman animals. If one would now go on to assert that animals can be experimented upon, one is begging this discussion's question by merely stipulating which entitlements animals in fact possess or lack. The superiority claim is not

[9] H. T. Engelhardt, Jr., "Animals: Their Right to Be Used," in *Why Animal Experimentation Matters: The Use of Animals in Medical Research*, ed. E. F. Paul and J. Paul, 175–96 (New Brunswick: Transaction Publishers, 2001), 182.

[10] 1994: 256. Cohen, "The Case for the Use of Animals in Biomedical Research," 156. For specific criticism of Cohen's argument, see Cavalieri, *The Animal Question*, 77–78; DeGrazia, *Taking Animals Seriously*, 36–37; and Nobis, "Carl Cohen's 'Kind' Argument."

[11] I will not enter the question whether the degrees view is defensible (if it is not, the superiority argument above is to be dismissed). For some arguments against levels of moral considerability see, for example, Rowland, *Animals Like Us*, chaps. 2–3; DeGrazia, *Taking Animals Seriously*, chap. 3; Regan, *The Case for Animal Rights*, chap. 7.2.

question-begging. It strives to show some linkage between the more in-clusive protections humans have and the permissibility of experiments. Yet where and how can one locate such a linkage? Short of self-defense—and experimentation on animals is not a form of self-defense—the scope of one's own protections never extends to the permissibility of harming others.

An alternative rendering of "degrees" and "value" that does not beg our question would appeal to some vague sense of "worth": we are "more valuable" than they are, hence we may experiment on them. Yet being endowed with some higher "value"—allow the upholder of this defense to leave the content of "value" open—does not permit the more valuable entity to harm beings of lower value. Nor does superior value connect smoothly with having more protection than entities possessing inferior value. It is conceivable to have beings of "lower worth" covered by protections that are similar to, or even greater than, those extended to beings of a higher value. An obtuse capitalist may emphatically assert that disabled individuals are less valuable than healthy and highly pro-ductive ones yet still see society as obliged to extend more inclusive pro-tections to disabled individuals. So what can plausibly correlate value with levels of protection?

To clarify the point I am attacking, I present the argument that to my mind unnecessarily bewitches pro-animal philosophers into arguing for equal considerability. Admitting dissimilar "status," they fear, will make the following reasoning sound:

1. Humans are worthier than animals.
2. The greater value of humans over animals *just means* or *entails* extending limited protection to animals.
3. "Limited protection" *means* that some actions that ought not be done to humans can be directed at animals (even if the latter are eligible for some moral protection), and this can be done if a substantial justification is supplied and some worthy cause is specified.

In the context of the ethics of research, it would now follow that:

4. Using animals in research presents a worthy cause: it exhibits the right virtues and promotes overall good consequences both to people and to some animals.
5. Conclusion: animal use in research is justified.

I reject (2) above. We tend to think that (2) is plausible for three reasons: first, similar status has been repeatedly *correlated* with sharing identical protections, hence it seems reasonable to associate dissimilar status with different protections. Second, arguing for lower considerability has been repeatedly used (rather, misused) to excuse extending only limited protection. Third, no protection can be granted to beings that are not eligible for even minimal moral protection; technically put, possessing moral status seems to be both a necessary and a sufficient condition for some level of protection. It therefore seems natural to suppose that there is some correlation between higher status and more entitlements. These claims can be accepted as true (ignoring the confusions that "moral status" introduces), but they do not support (2), namely, it does not follow that *degrees* of rights or other protections derive from degrees of moral status. The flaw is the move from protections being derived from status to *levels* of protection being derived from (or dependent on) levels of moral status. A club that has regular and honorary members can extend special rights to honorary members, and honorary membership can just mean special rights. But it is an open question whether it should mean this. Honorary membership can simply have symbolic significance: it can even mean that the club expects more from honorary members, that they have more obligations and less entitlements than regular members. Greater status does not just mean (nor does it entail) more rights or more protection. To conclude: if one grants animals even minimal moral protection, then no "threshold" that humans pass validates experimenting on animals since nothing in having high moral status as such hooks on to placing or removing specific restrictions. The human superiority argument as an apology for research must be wrong.

A possible objection here is to say something like this: "It may be the case that the degrees of protection are not necessarily derived from degrees of status. But is it not reasonable to expect that considerations underlying determining degrees of protection should include the degree of moral status of the entities involved? Weaker glue than logical necessity can legitimately solder distinct evaluations. Accordingly, exposing a logical disconnection between degrees of moral status and degrees of protection does not suffice." Yet the gap I am foregrounding is not merely logical. Nothing makes the move from status to degrees of protection factually reasonable or morally probable. High moral status can be linked with greater protection, but it can just as easily entail greater moral demands, such as refusing to sacrifice entities of lower status for one's own gain. What makes one connection more reasonable than the other?

"But surely," a different objector will say, "the higher status and superior value you are willing to grant us humans minimally means that in us-or-them cases—like pressing cases in animal-based research—entities of lower status should be sacrificed first." The problem here is the repetition of the flaw we found in the cruder version of the superiority claim: the greater value of A over B does not justify A in *doing* anything to B. True, if it is a matter of saving either A or B, then it is justified to save A, which is why, upon entering a burning house and having the option of saving a sick old man or his healthy eight young dogs (Peter Carruthers's example), it is justified to save the man. But here the person doing the saving is not doing anything to B, but to A, and is simply not intervening in B's situation. Dilemmas pertaining to humans alone elicit similar intuitions: if I enter a burning plane and can either save a scientist about to devise an important vaccine or the man sitting at her side, it is acceptable to save the scientist. Note though, that in such examples the justifications do not depend on considerations of value: say I save a woman rather than a man because I happen to prefer women to men. The "saving" scenario justifies many such choices (or let us say this: unless my saving action is predicated on a bias that is itself deemed immoral, I shall probably not be blamed for acting upon such preferences).

But research raises a different question entirely: Is it justified to sacrifice these dogs in order to save the old man or to improve his quality of life? Here one is not merely *refraining* from action but actively harming the less valuable entities. Consider the thought-experiments designed to embarrass utilitarians: no one has an easy time saying that it is right to harvest organs from an individual who has a negative or neutral effect on society if this can save an important scientist. Opposing such harvesting does not stem merely from slippery-slope concerns, or our concern with rights, or our interest to limit the invasive power of institutions. Apart from these, there is the basic flaw of the reasoning: my having an inferior value relative to some other being, even if such inferiority can be established, does not justify anyone in *doing* anything to me. And we tend to miss this because we confuse it with the similar case, which is justified, of aiding the being that we value more, but not doing anything detrimental to the being that we value less.[12] This argument relies on a purely formal structure: B's inferiority relative to A does not justify anyone in harming B in order to benefit A. Nothing in the argument depends on the inferior entity being human. There is, then, no way of limiting this reasoning to humans.[13]

---

[12] H. LaFollette and N. Shanks, *Brute Science: Dilemmas of Animal Experimentation* (London: Routledge, 1996), 251–52, identify a further moral principle that is being infringed by experiments: "acts versus omissions." Experimentation involves harming animals rather than not intervening in the situation of sick humans. In the standard application of moral principles, actively hurting someone is worse than not helping someone who needs help.

[13] The "us or them" scenarios above thus conflate legitimate bias and immoral conduct since the cases in these examples involve acting versus noninterference. Legitimate preference can involve activity that benefits the favored party and does not interfere with the situation of the other party. But some situations are more complex. Jamieson and Regan, in "On the Ethics of the Use of Animals in Research," present a thought-experiment designed to undercut what I have just said. A terrorist seated at a tank is executing dozens of

A final objection is consequentialist: if it is granted that A is of superior value to B, and if—as consequentialists hold—maximizing value ought to govern all our moral transactions, then the superiority claim successfully shows that curtailing the interests of animals by experimenting on them is morally justified if it promotes the well-being of the more valuable humans, thereby maximizing overall utility. Three types of arguments oppose this objection. The first is the set of general objections to consequentialism as such (which I shall not rehash here). Second, since some of our most radical pro-animal arguments are couched in utilitarian considerations, we may well suspect that once we begin probing further what "value" and "maximizing" it should plausibly mean, we will reach precisely the kind of morally relevant properties that have induced utilitarians like Bentham or Singer to demand a radical reform of animal-related practice, rather than reconfirm the existing status quo. Third, assume that our consequentialist presents a variant of consequentialism that does not entail reform and that utilizes the superiority claim to justify research. To avoid the implication that not only animals but humans too can be experimented upon should experimenting on a small number of them contribute to the welfare of numerous others, the consequentialist will need to add some restrictions regarding what may be done to humans in a just society, even if the disutility of harming them is offset by benefiting many others. Yet establishing this limitation on consequentialist grounds alone is not easy. True, if people know that it is permissible to experiment on them without their consent, this in itself diminishes the overall good in a substantial way when factoring in the disutility of the now widespread anxiety of every person: that ghoulish possibility that he or she will happen to play a part in some such a gruesome scenario. But such anxieties can be quantified, measured against, and offset by the much more severe and palpable suffering induced by some disease. The consequentialist will have to concede that if no feasible alternative to deploying human subjects for some diseases is forthcoming, it is morally permissible to do so on the grounds that the value of many individuals surpasses the value of few human subjects.[14]

---

hostages. Stopping him requires blowing up the tank, to which the terrorist has tied up a young girl. Say that we know for sure that the girl will not be harmed after the executions stop, and we allow that the value of the lives of ten people is greater than the value of the life of the girl. To use the terms above, in this thought-experiment one is morally required to actively harm B in order to benefit A. To conceptualize the moral justification of research along these lines (a direction that Jamieson and Regan reject) in effect amounts to saying that research is the lesser of two evils. I postpone discussion of this particular justification to a later section in this chapter.

[14] See, in this context, Frey's previously cited discussion in "Vivisection, Morals and Medicine."

This does not yet mean that it is wrong to sacrifice animals for the benefits that research offers. The conclusion is merely that we cannot exonerate such practice by appealing to the inferior value of animals.

THE ARGUMENT FROM GREATER CARE

The cruder manner by which the greater care for humans excuses research is through questions like: "What would you say if the sick person is your child, and saving her requires sacrificing animals?" Here is psychiatrist Robert White's less polemically pitched, nonhypothetical version of this claim:

> We wept and watched, my wife and I, as a little girl fought for her life. She was tiny, frail, helpless, and so very vulnerable. Motionless except as her chest rose and fell spasmodically, there lay Lauren, our first grandchild, born so prematurely that each breath was a desperate and failing effort. We wept, our hearts torn by the growing realization that Lauren might not live. The next day she died. The research on baby lambs and kittens that has given life to many premature infants such as Lauren was still in the future and would come too late for her.
>
> In time, two grandsons, Jonathan and Bryan, were born. Premature babies, they also had to struggle for life. Our pain of uncertainty and of waiting was all to be endured twice again. But the little boys lived. The knowledge gained through research on lambs and kittens gave them life, a gift that Lauren could not have.[15]

The philosophical problem with such moving confessions when they mobilize provivisection arguments is that this kind of reasoning permits too much and is not limited to animals. People will steal, lie, and kill to save their loved ones. And so a willingness to do this or that to someone else to save one's child or grandchild attests to the strength of parental commitment rather than forming a moral justification.

The argument from care appeals to the truism that we simply care more for humans or for our loved ones. Sometimes it is added that since humans are more valuable, we *ought* to care more about them, which is why research that saves humans or improves their quality of life at the expense of animals is justified. Mary Midgley and, more recently, B. A. Brody, who have presented variants of this argument from species solidarity, have labored hard to establish a distinction between partiality (which may be good, say, preferring one's family over strangers) and

---

[15] R. B. White, "Contested Terrain: Beastly Questions," *The Hastings Center Report* 19 (2) (March 1989): 39.

discrimination (which is always bad). Midgley's claims have been criti-
cized in detail by DeGrazia, and Brody confesses that he has not successfully established this distinction, so it is not obvious that an updated
contemporary variant of this position exists.[16] But aside from the viability of successfully distinguishing between legitimate and dubious biases,
the deeper flaw here resembles the fallacy involved in the justification
from the greater value of humans. The argument moves from our greater
care for and attachment to humans (that jointly support discounting animal interests relative to human ones), to justifying sacrificing animals
for the sake of human welfare. This reasoning, as S. F. Sapontzis (1988)
notes, is unsound: caring more for A than for B justifies benefiting A
before B (relieving human hunger outweighs relieving animal hunger).
But greater care for A cannot justify harming B. Like the argument
from superiority, the reasoning from greater care or natural sentiment to
justifying harm conflates benefiting humans over animals (which makes
sense when one values them more than animals or cares more for them)
with actively hurting animals to benefit humans (which is not justified).
Human-human morality recognizes this distinction all the time: citizens
care more for the poor in their own country than the poor of other na-
tions even if the latter suffer more, and this excuses them aiding the former before assisting the latter (in technical terms, they are "discounting"
the interests of some humans relative to those of others). But countries
that harm other countries to benefit their own citizens are condemned.

Thought-experiments designed to embarrass pro-animal philosophers
into accepting the need to sometimes actively harm animals, thus exposing the higher value of humans ("Would you pitch a dog or a human
overboard to save the survivors in a lifeboat?") fail, first, because they do
not prove lower value (as we saw, even if they did prove this, no proresearch result follows), and second, because they do not amount to a
moral justification: Ann may prove just as willing to throw Suzan's children overboard to save her own children, yet that shows neither that
Suzan's children are less valuable, nor that this action is morally sound.[17]

Provivisection literature also includes a survival-based variant on the
argument from greater care. Research, in this variant, is a manifestation
of the evolutionary imperative for species survival, and for the apologists
of animal experiments this turns into a moral justification:

> The foregoing arguments in this essay [arguments according to
> which animal-based research promotes human survival] illustrate

---

[16] M. Midgley, *Animals and Why They Matter* (Athens: University of Georgia Press,
1983); Brody, "Defending Animal Research"; DeGrazia, *Taking Animals Seriously*, 63–65.
[17] Can research be conceptualized as a lifeboat situation? For some relevant disanalogies, see Finsen, "Sinking the Research Lifeboat."

that, from the perspective of Darwinian theory, the exploitation of some species of animals by others is not an appropriate topic for moral concern, especially when the exploiting animals need to engage in this activity in order to survive. This generalization applies to the human animals as well as to other predatory species.[18]

As a biologist . . . I recognize that all species are in a struggle for existence. As the most intelligent species on the planet, we would be extremely foolish to deny this fact and not act on behalf of our own families, friends, and, ultimately, our own species by not engaging in biomedical research by all means available. Actually, we would be denying a biological imperative: the drive to survive.[19]

Philosophers who would attempt to recast such arguments in ways that do not rely on obvious conflation of descriptive and normative claims will have to turn survival into a morally acceptable motive for action. "Denying biological imperatives" as such will not do (that opens a Pandora's box since culture and moral conduct is largely built on numerous such denials). The implicit principle that these authors rely on is that acting out one's preprogrammed blueprint is on its own a moral justification for one's actions. This principle is patently false, since one may be programmed to do evil. And since these authors do not also endorse determinism, they cannot be understood as saying that we have no choice in the matter but to act out our instincts, thereby exonerating our animal-related practices.

Survival is itself a morally complex motive. Fierce survival struggles sometimes (though not always) altogether annul moral consideration. We shun the presumption to morally criticize the actions of starving or terrorized people. On the other hand, some who have survived Nazi ghettos, for example, have been put on trial for surviving through corrupt means. Various war crimes also attest to our willingness to place moral blame on those whose personal survival was severely threatened when performing the crimes. Personal survival does not then trump all moral concerns. Even if it did, the theorists I am citing are not discussing personal survival but the survival of the species. This is far-fetched. I am not aware of an animal-related scientific breakthrough that is credited with saving our entire species as such. If we ever reach an impasse that requires animal experiments to save human existence, survival through such sacrifice can be conceptualized through Darwinian amoral terms

---

[18] Nicoll and Russell, "A Darwinian View of the Issues Associated with the Use of Animals in Biomedical Research," in *Why Animal Experimentation Matters: The Use of Animals in Medical Research*, ed. E. F. Paul and J. Paul, 168 (New Brunswick: Transaction Publishers, 2001).

[19] Morrison, "Ethical Principles," 105.

(note, though, that the same justification holds for experimenting on humans of a particular ethnic group or blood type). Impending, hitherto unknown destructive viruses, bacteria, protozoans, and parasites can possibly lead to our extinction. But such doomsday scenarios do not support continuing research, but merely preserving the theory and small-scale practice that is devoted specifically to these potential calamities. If such threats should genuinely motivate our animal-related research, the implication is also that the vast majority of these experiments (product testing, basic science, most of genetics) should be immediately discontinued in their animal-based forms, since they are unrelated to these microscopic future disasters (indeed, they could well lead into them, by artificially creating unknown life-forms). Nuclear disarmament seems a better possibility on which these survival-motivated scientists should focus.

We care more for the survival and welfare of our fellow humans than the continuation and comfort of nonhumans. This is a description of our psychology, about what we value more and less, evaluations that themselves may issue from deeper biological imperatives. I argued that *pace* the evolutionary excuses above, these evaluations have no probative force precisely because they seem to be merely built-in constituents, rather than sifted evaluations. Moreover, I argued that even if they were sifted evaluations, as authors like Midgley, Brody, or Francis and Norman try to show, they would still not vindicate harming others.[20] Nepotism shows that our feeling of closeness to some individuals does not justify harming or exploiting those whom we value less. Discounting animal interests, even if it is morally permissible to discount them, would not justify research.

Humans Deserve More

Unequal treatment is sometimes excused by appealing to greater desert. Such arguments are typically entangled with claims of the relative superiority of human over nonhuman animals that we evaluated previously. But unlike mere assertions of greater importance, here the tacit reasoning appeals to considerations of greater desert:

> Any consideration of suffering must lead us to the conclusion that regard for the interests of different species must be differentiated, following the criterion of "like suffering," according to the degree of

---

[20] Midgley, *Animals and Why They Matter*; Brody, "Defending Animal Research"; L. P. Francis and R. Norman, "Some Animals Are More Equal Than Others," *Philosophy* 53 (1978): 507–27.

their mental capacity, i.e., of their capacity for suffering. . . . it follows that we should give earnest consideration to the interests of *all* sentient beings but that we should give *more* consideration to the interests of those species with the greatest mental complexity.[21]

[C]ertain capacities, which seem to be unique to human beings, *entitle their possessors to a privileged position in the moral community*. Both rats and human beings dislike pain, and so we have a *prima facie* reason not to inflict pain on either. But if we can free human beings from crippling diseases, pain and death through experimentation . . . then I think that such experimentation is justified because human lives are more valuable than animal lives.[22]

If A and B are children quarrelling over a piece of pie, and B already had some of the pie, A *deserves* a larger piece of it now and should get it even if B will eat a smaller piece. Experimentation on animals is sometimes defended in this way, the argument being that since humans in some unspecified sense "deserve more" (to deploy the references above: human suffering is to be accorded greater weight, and so the human interest in escaping suffering overrides the animal's interest in avoiding pain), sacrificing animals to save humans or relieve their suffering is justified. Yet this reasoning is unsound. The logic that underlies research is different from unequal allocation of pieces of pie, and this difference undermines the argument from greater desert as a vindication of research. Something that B possesses (its life) is *taken* from it, to respond to A's need. Here there is no question of distributing unequally a shared resource. The question is one of dispossession. Even if we take the strongest scenario on behalf of experimentation with animals, a life versus a life, the moral logic of the reasoning is dubious: say that A deserves something that he has in a greater degree than B deserves to have his. Does this justify *taking* what B has to preserve A?

Examples of such moves in human-human morality suggest that when dispossession on behalf of greater desert has been conducted—for example, uprisings that involved dispossession of nobility—this has sometimes been rationalized through deflating the nobility's right of ownership. Since no one thinks that animals do not deserve the lives that they have— to the extent that this formulation even makes sense—this justification cannot apply to animals. When the right of ownership is fully recognized in human-human morality and the argument from desert is invoked to

---

[21] Preece and Chamberlain, *Animal Welfare and Human Values*, 53–54. While this is precisely the kind of reasoning I mean to examine shortly, it is not clear whether Preece and Chamberlain themselves see it as the basis of justifying research as such.

[22] B. Steinbock, "Speciesism and the Idea of Equality," *Philosophy* (1978): 253–54 (emphasis mine).

vindicate actively taking something from someone, dispossession is typically rationalized via considerations of fairness—for example, taking from the rich to benefit the poor through unequal taxation practices. There are prudential considerations for doing this. But the standard moral justification of unequal taxation and unequal allocation of funds aimed at benefiting the poor is that such assists the children of the poor to compete with the children of the rich from a fairer starting point. The overall justification appeals to benefiting the weaker party at the expense of the stronger one. Obviously, this move cannot justify research, since unlike unequal taxation here the weak benefit the strong. In addition, redistribution of wealth has its limits: one can take from the rich only so much. The underlying moral principle is that the benefactor cannot end up worse off than the beneficiary. Research violates this principle too since the animals end up dead.

To conclude: even when conceding the strongest case for research, in which sacrificing an animal positively saves a human life, the animal has been made worse off than the human. Excusing this outcome by contending that humans deserve more than animals is undercut by violating the moral principles that underlie acceptable applications of the justification from greater desert. Such justifications rely either on deflating ownership rights of the party being dispossessed or on benefiting the weak at the expense of the strong, and avoiding making the giver worse off than the receiver. Neither of these applies in the case of research.

But is it reasonable to extrapolate from human-human morality to human-animal morality? Imagine a critic saying this: "Even if the logic of greater moral desert does not carry over smoothly from humans to animals, this proves nothing. It is hardly surprising that such moves work differently in human moral contexts than when one is thinking about animals. But nothing important is to be inferred from this trivial and expected fact. Animals should be sacrificed to save humans because humans deserve more. Happily, analogous reasoning from greater desert cannot be applied to humans, but research on animals is a different matter and should go on." This objection is convincing only until one recognizes that it cannot be restricted to an apology for animal-based research. It can, for example, unproblematically be used by someone who would like to torture animals: "In human-human contexts," the sadist will say, "we regard as basic the need to avoid cruel actions that harm others in order to derive pleasure. But why should we be anthropocentric and suppose that "harming" or "deriving pleasure" or "cruelty" retain their meaning or "moral logic" when one moves from humans to animals? One should not be cruel to humans but may direct cruelty to animals, so long as one will not turn to look for human victims later." The numerous differences between sadists and scientists should not

obfuscate the manner by which the objection we are scrutinizing now recycles the same improbable move: if research advocates may appeal to a
discrepancy between human and animal-related application of moral
terms, sadists can do so too.

In response, my opponent will reinvoke the degrees view of moral considerability we encountered earlier: animals have some moral standing,
enough to safeguard them against sadism, but not enough to prevent
experiments, and this is because "humans deserve more." My argument
regarding the usual moral logic of greater desert cannot then carry over
from human to nonhuman contexts as I tried to do, since my human examples concerned subjects of identical moral standing, whereas the move
to entities of lesser status modifies the probable application of such
terms. But the problem with this countermove is that it recycles the same
reasoning that failed above when trying to justify research through
greater importance. Lesser moral standing does not hook onto lesser protection or its equivalent, "greater desert," since no argumentative links
bind degrees of moral standing (or degrees of "desert") with particular
conduct restrictions.

Preventing Harm

The argument from the benefits of experiments is the most commonly
used justification for research:

> Research in neuroscience contributes significantly to society by in-
> creasing our understanding of the brain, its organization and func-
> tion. Knowledge generated by neuroscience research has led to
> important advances in the understanding of diseases and disorders
> that affect the nervous system and to the development of better treat-
> ments which reduce suffering. Continued progress in many areas of
> neuroscience research requires the use of living animals to investigate
> the complex systems and functions of the nervous system because no
> adequate alternatives exist. Therefore, the Society for Neuroscience
> has taken the position that the use of living animals in properly de-
> signed scientific research is both ethical and appropriate.[23]

The claim is that if we stop animal dependent basic research, in vivo
applied research, medicine testing, and toxicity testing of potentially
harmful chemicals to which we are routinely exposed, a direct leap from

---

[23] Cited from "Introduction," in *Handbook for the Use of Animals in Research*, published in 1997 by the Society for Neuroscience. Available at http://web.sfn.org. The author
is not identified.

non-animal-based research (in vitro–based research, computerized mathematical models, diagnostic imaging, epidemiology-oriented research, and other alternatives) to humans would harm many more humans than a system in which such drugs are also pretested through the intermediary stage of animal experiments. Animal tests constitute a stage that screens out numerous drugs that will harm the first human recipients of the drug. The same holds for gradual perfection of invasive techniques (artificial heart valves, open-heart surgery, transplants), which have all been devised through years of testing on animals. True, requiring in vivo sifting also leads to missing important drugs that benefit people and harm rodents. But given the alternative, we would rather not try on ourselves drugs that debilitate guinea pigs, even if there is a chance that these will benefit us.

There are four familiar problems with this argument. The first is that it justifies too little as it is relevant only to a narrow subsection of applied research (drug development and drug testing).[24] Basic research does not save lives, and nonmedical product testing is many times unnecessary (is it, for example, nothing less than "necessary" to examine whether a new brand of brake fluid is toxic or not? Is it "necessary" to develop and test new brands of products that already exist in large variety?). Admittedly, no one can predict what basic experiments will be instrumental for future applied research. But this is a shaky excuse, as one is no longer killing animals to save humans, but is doing so for the mere chance of saving humans. This places scientists in a difficult spot: they have to show a sufficient number of cases in which basic and applied results were not only correlated, but causally linked. Defenders of vivisection have bitten the bullet here, citing examples such as the development of insulin or Pasteur's discovery of vaccination.[25] Yet it is far from obvious that these dazzling highlights of medical advance at its best are indicative of routine experimental practice. More important, scientists have to accept the implication of the reduction of basic into applied research, that is, experiments that cannot affect any kind of illness, those that merely advance scientific knowledge (say, understanding minute aspects of a neurological process that is unrelated to any known human illness), will lose their justification. Claiming that one never knows how these advances will possibly be harnessed to applied medical advances seems evasive. Morally, such a claim is on the same footing as recommending routine torture to all convicted felons to gain information regarding future possible crimes: that such a practice may bear positive fruits does not vindicate it.

[24] For some statistics, see the notes below.
[25] J. H. Botting and A. R. Morrison, "Animal Research Is Vital to Medicine," *Scientific American* 276 (2) (February 1997): 67–69.

The first problem with this argument then, is that for anyone who accepts the justification from medical necessity, there is also the severe limitation of nonmedically oriented research. Second, R. G. Frey argues that if benefits "outweigh" harms, it is difficult to see why experimentation is to be limited only to animals.[26] Secular attempts to unpack the "sanctity" of human life, a notion that could set a morally meaningful difference between human and nonhuman animals, appeal to the rich content human life has. But such characterization entails that a human life of very poor quality qualifies as a legitimate object for research. Third, if benefiting humans is what we are after, if relieving sickness and human suffering is our genuine moral motivation, we should allocate funds to third-world sufferers rather than to animal-based research, which is targeted at such a narrow group of humans.[27] Fourth, there are problems with deriving humanly applicable, medically solid results from experiments conducted on animals. It has been urged that scientists have greatly exaggerated the importance of such experiments for human welfare.[28] The charge is threefold: first, detailed perusal of specific therapeutic breakthroughs in the scientific literature suggests that clinical investigation and insight rather than animal experiments played the decisive role (and when experiments did play a causal role, these could have been replaced with non-animal-based models yielding the same results). Second, advocates of experiments have been charged with conflating the *correlation* of all successful medication with experimenting on animals (which is a legal requirement) and the *causal* claim that such experiments were a necessary stage for such development. Third, there is the methodological problem of relevance: aspirin kills cats, penicillin kills guinea pigs—both help humans. On the other hand, thalidomide is teratogenic for humans but harmless to many animals. Establishing that a drug benefits humans requires clinical studies on humans. Experiments on animals lead us both to miss beneficial drugs and to use harmful ones. And saying that pretesting on animals prevents disasters on humans is true only if one also admits that the existence of such a stage may involve missing life-saving drugs. The overall utility (for humans)

---

[26] Frey, "Vivisection, Morals and Medicine."

[27] Singer and Ryder have made this argument. For an in-depth analysis and criticism of various replies to it, see C. K. Fink, "Animal Experimentation and the Argument from Limited Resources," *Between the Species* 7 (2) (Spring 1991): 90–95. I have my doubts about this particular argument ("the argument from limited resources") since it seems to conflate right and supererogatory action, implausibly implying that one should avoid good when one can do even better.

[28] LaFollette and Shanks, *Brute Science*, chap. 2; C. R. Greek and J. S. Greek, *Sacred Cows and Golden Geese: The Human Cost of Experimenting on Animals* (London: Continuum, 2000).

of pretesting on animals is then debatable, and the methodological necessity of the animal experiment stage is scientifically (not merely
morally) doubtful.[29]

My training does not permit me to appraise the literature on alternatives to animal-based experiments, so I cannot evaluate the argument on
behalf of the disutility for humans of such experiments. The problem is
not merely that I am not a scientist. Since mastering each of the alternatives requires detailed expertise, no single scientist can confidently assess
such claims, whether she is pro or against alternatives (and this indicates
the need for incorporating different experts in the ethical committees authorizing research).[30] But the moral (as distinct from the prudential) side

[29] Botting and Morrison, in "Animal Research Is Vital to Medicine," argue against these
examples, basically saying that better testing on animals would have prevented these disanalogies. Rachels, in *Created from Animals*, 220, has formulated a relevant dilemma that
haunts scientific justifications of research: to justify the scientific validity of the extrapola-
tion from animals to humans, scientists have to emphasize similarities between humans and
animals. But to establish the moral justification of the practice, scientists need to emphasize
the differences between human and nonhuman animals. I think that Rachels is wrong, as
there is no inconsistency in holding that a being is physiologically similar to another one,
but morally very different from it. Physiological similarity (think of humans and the larger
apes) may still give rise to radically dissimilar capacities, and these (rather than physiological considerations alone) may be deemed as the morally relevant properties.

[30] I will say more about alternatives later in this chapter. For a succinct exposition of the
state of alternatives and some figures regarding funding of alternatives (true to 1997), see
M. Mukerjee, "Trends in Animal Research," *Scientific American* 276 (2) (February 1997):
70–77. Aside from human utility or disutility, economic considerations that are raised
by the literature against research actually play for both sides: on the one hand, antivivisectionists repeatedly claim that the lab-animal industry is a big business, providing jobs to
numerous technicians, veterinarians, cage manufacturers, and so forth, and so there is a
substantial nonscientific vested interest to continue experimentation even when potential
alternatives are suggested. The combination of this professional and financial interest, with
the legal requirements for extensive prehuman testing and the legislative restrictions that
pharmaceutical companies need to comply with, along with the conformity of scientists
trained in specific methods themselves required to comply with publication demands for
in vivo results, leads to a systematic suppression of deeper and braver policies regarding allocation of research funds. On the other hand, scientists I talked to say that in vitro experiments and other alternatives are both known and much cheaper than experimenting on
animals (cf. Dolan, *Ethics, Animals and Science*, 177). A. Coghlan, ("Animal Experimentation on Trial," *New Scientist* 176 (2370) (November 2002): 16), claims that monkeys for
experiments cost seven thousand dollars each, and so there is a built-in institutional motivation to decrease the number of animals used and killed (which leads some institutes, such
as Israel's Weizmann Institute of Science, to practice informal sharing of killed animals by
several researchers). If such techniques are indeed cheaper, and if, as antivivisection literature holds, using them rather than rodents is scientifically sounder, the scientific argument
on behalf of the antivivisection camp is actually deflated. Soon we will reach a stage in
which the intermediary step from glass to animals would be exposed as unnecessary, since
whatever is gained from the in vivo stage will be successfully predicted by the initial non-
animal-based techniques.

of the matter is different from these considerations. If animals have some kind of moral standing, we cannot simply say that morality is reducible to overall utility for humans alone. When this limitation is recognized, it is possible that the moral case against vivisection will admit that experiments benefit humans while being immoral. Gaining from a practice is simply beside the moral point. "Organized crime," a cynical critic might say, "is an example of a large-scale immoral practice that benefits some, yet the Mafia never pretends that prudential benefits constitute a moral defense. Why should the benefits of science to humans count higher on the moral ladder?" Of course, even if animal and human victims have the same moral standing, one disanalogy between the Mafia and science is that the former is a self-serving enterprise interested in promoting the welfare of some, while science benefits everyone. But in the new context of interspecies ethics, the cynic has a genuine and disturbing point. Who is "everyone"? He would press to know. "Do rodents benefit from research? And if they do not, what sets a meaningful moral difference between the violence involved in types of self-serving actions that we condemn, and violence which we justify? Is it merely a matter of where 'we' are situated? Wasn't the slave-trade based precisely upon such reasoning?"

Harming humans should experimentation stop is not, then, a morally viable factor when assessing the moral status of animal-based research. Morally correct action can be imprudent; prudent action might be immoral. Doing the right thing sometimes carries a cost in human lives and may increase human suffering. Consider now a subtler variation of this argument.

THE LESSER OF TWO EVILS

Say that experimenting on animals is immoral. Should it stop? Two arguments suggest that it should not. The first is that when the prudential benefits of experimentation are not denied, the immorality involved may be considered as a "regrettable necessity" or a "necessary evil" (this is a variant of the argument considered above) or a "lifeboat situation." And since the immoral practice furthers knowledge and therapeutic capacity and is not directed at some morally dubious end, such research should continue given the strong prudential reasons that support it. The claims of science versus the claims of animals are not a simple case of morality versus prudence. Reprehensible examples of the latter clash, from Plato's ring of Gyges on, involve egoistic benefits rather than the ones science provides. Unlike self-serving acts, in this specific clash, prudence—if therapy is mere prudence—should override morality. Practical reasoning does not include only moral considerations, and in this particular case, practical reasoning should lead us to support research, even if it is immoral. There are other examples—e.g., some strategic decisions in wartime—wherein complex decisions involve an interplay between moral and nonmoral considerations, the latter overriding the former. A military decision maker led by moral considerations alone will probably be making some wrong decisions.[31]

Apart from the argument from practical reasoning, a different argument that supports research while acknowledging its nonmoral nature rests on a distinction between immoral and nonmoral actions. Stealing food from a starving person is immoral. When the person doing the stealing is himself starving, the action is still immoral, but few will blame the thief. The inability to blame results both from considerations of empathy (in the sense that people realize that if they were starving, they would resort to the same actions) and from the situation being one of necessity: due to the either-or nature of the act and the compulsion to choose the lesser of two evils. Call such actions "nonmoral." The ability or inability to blame the person doing the dubious action ("inability to blame" in the sense above) is partly what sets the difference between nonmoral and immoral actions. Experimentation that saves lives at the expense of animals can be claimed to be in this sense "nonmoral" rather than "immoral": it involves an either-or situation and is designed to prevent a weighty harm. No one who cares for a relative afflicted with an incurable illness can be blamed if she supports animal-dependent research. Can we then likewise say that the use of experimental animals is not desirable but is acceptable?[32]

Both arguments articulate the same line: we sometimes accept immoral conduct. But the disanalogy between plausible applications of these arguments and the specific issue of experimenting on animals arises upon perusing the cases in human-human morality where "lesser of two evil" arguments are in fact accepted. In human-human morality, immoral conduct can be excused in cases where (a) the action has no feasible alternatives that generate less harm, (b) the person performing the immoral act has searched hard for these alternatives, even if such were not

---

[31] I am thinking here of a model of practical reasoning such as the one presented by Eugene Garver in his *Aristotle's Rhetoric: An Art of Character* (Chicago: University of Chicago Press, 1994), in which practical reasoning on a complex matter involves considering (a) whether a course of action is honorable, (b) whether it is prudential, and (c) whether it is just. A decision maker can obviously make a mistake in one of these areas. But the force of the model is that a common mistake relates to simply ignoring one of them altogether. People who consider nothing but expedience, or nothing but justice, are exercising incomplete practical reasoning.

[32] E.g., with Dolan, *Ethics, Animals and Science*, 214.

ultimately discovered, (c) the act is necessary in the sense that not acting in the immoral way is likely to imply some great harm, (d) the action involves the agent's recognition regarding the immoral nature of the act, a recognition manifested through remorse or a willingness to compensate the victim (one cannot, for example, be jovial or indifferent when performing the act), and (e) one looks hard for ways of minimizing the harm done during and after the action.

Current scientific practice does not come near to respecting (a)–(e). Western legal systems and the inner restrictions imposed by research institutions in most countries now recognize some version of the three-R approach. Demanding scientists to submit a cost-benefit analysis justifying the number, manner, and kind of animals used for experiments is also popular. But it is difficult to know whether such steps make a genuine difference since a crucial variant here is the degree of leniency of the authorizing bodies. One researcher told me that any scientist that knows math can manipulate the figures of a cost-benefit analysis in order to get any number of animals approved (determining the precise number of animals that are approved for use in a particular experiment depends on factors like expected number of failures both in the experiment and in the process of obtaining the desired type of animal tissue; such a figure can be adjusted to justify using more or less animals). Then there is the question of enforcement. The number of animals used in experiments in the United States suggests that the implementation of the first R, replacement, is not too strict.[33] According to one estimate concerned with worldwide fund allocations, we are still below devoting 1 percent of our overall research funding to developing alternatives, a figure that undermines our capacity to genuinely invoke "necessary evil" formulations.[34] As for avoiding great harm, the extent of research is vast—the number of animals killed yearly in the United States alone

[33] Dolan (ibid.) and Webster (*Animal Welfare*) give figures suggesting that the Animals (Scientific Procedures) Act of 1986 has dramatically reduced the number of animals used in the UK. As for the United States, D. Rudacille, *The Scalpel and the Butterfly: The Conflict between Animal Research and Animal Protection* (Berkeley: University of California Press, 2000), 294–313, does not see any decrease in these numbers as one would have expected if replacement had become substantial. Based on figures culled from the NIH, USDA, and others, Mukerjee ("Trends in Animal Research," 75) declares that without doubt the number of animals used in research has dropped by half from the 1970s on the Continent. Yet the figures given in the graphs in that essay do not support this assertion. Clear assessment is difficult as increase or decrease in numbers may result from causes that have nothing to do with tighter controls (e.g., changes in preferred models within the community of experimenters can dramatically diminish or increase numbers).

[34] This figure was presented by Sara Amundson (Doris Day Animal League) in a talk at the 5th World Congress on Alternatives and Animal Use in the Life Sciences, Berlin, 2005.

reaches tens of millions[35]—and only a small percentage of animals killed are related in any way to preventing an impending great harm (most basic research is regulated by the need to know rather than the need to save or cure).[36] As I said, there have been strong criticisms against the results of applied experiments in the most pressing human illnesses,[37] and so even in this smaller group there is room for skepticism and for introducing a further range of controls to sift the effective experiments from ones that can be avoided.

As for minimizing harm to the victim, apart from loose usage of analgesia, euthanasia, and postoperative care, the requirement for controlled experiments with the least possible variants means that animals that survive one experiment are routinely killed since they cannot be used for another experiment (apart from scientific problems in multiple usage of animals, a reason frequently given for this is, ironically, the moral disinclination to experiment twice on an animal, a practice that obviously increases the overall number of animals that are subjected to experiments). One scientist told me that his specific research requires using a litter of

[35] It is not easy to determine how many animals die in research facilities. LaFollette and Shanks (*Brute Science*, vii) rely on statistics published by the American Medical Association in 1992, according to which 17–22 million animals are killed yearly in the United States. Rudacille (*The Scalpel and the Butterfly*, 303) gives a worldwide estimate of about 41 million animals per year. A glaringly different estimate is given by Jamieson and Regan ("On the Ethics of the Use of Animals in Science," 267), who speak of 200 million animals used (not necessarily killed) for scientific purposes in 1978 (their source being Diner's *Physical and Mental Suffering of Experimental Animals*). Finsen ("Sinking the Research Lifeboat") opens her paper with an estimate of 60–90 million animals killed yearly in the United States.

[36] Webster (*Animal Welfare*, 231) supplies a differentiation of research in the UK (1992) according to which scientific experiments make up 68.5 percent of animals experimented upon (and this number is divided into 47.1 percent that relate to "fundamental science: body functions and disease studies," 21.4 percent that are used as part of "applied science: development of drugs and other treatments"). If this breakdown is roughly indicative of the general proportion that applied experiments have, only one of every five animals is killed in an experiment that has a direct relation with disease. I did not manage to locate figures suggesting a further breakdown of this last category, indicative of the proportion of experiments that aim at developing medication to incurable illnesses (as opposed to, say, experiments aimed to produce more brands of medication that already exists or redundant—as opposed to nonredundant—repetitions of experiments). On the other hand, Preece and Chamberlain (*Animal Welfare and Human Values*, 67) give figures based mostly on *Nature* 346 (1990), according to which 50 percent of all animal experiments in 1989 were applied medical research. Of course, like many seemingly descriptive terms that make up this debate (e.g., the breakdown of pain into "mild," "moderate," and "severe"), the categories (e.g., "applied" vs. "basic," "disease-related") that make up such statistics cannot be accepted uncritically.

[37] On problems surrounding extrapolating results from animals to humans encountered by applied research in relation to AIDS, cancer, and cardiovascular disease, see Greek and Greek, *Sacred Cows and Golden Geese*, chaps. 8–10.

rats. His research can be conducted only with very young rats, but since the mother cannot be returned to the animal breeding facility after she has left it, and since she is needed for feeding the younger rats during the experiment, she has to be euthanized too. The killing of healthy animals after experiments is sometimes masked through distinguishing between animals "used" and animals "killed" as part of experiments. But since breeding facilities do not reuse animals that have exited the facility, a majority of animals that are used will be killed even if they do not die from the experiment. I found no statistics on or study of the scope of killing healthy animals in laboratories, and so I can only guess how widespread such killing is. Rehabilitating animals that have been experimented upon (sometimes called "the fourth R") is rarely practiced with regard to higher species (I have heard of projects involving rehabilitating or rehousing horses, dogs, cats, and monkeys). No project I know of addresses healthy rodents, which are the most commonly used subjects for experiments. To my mind, the practice of killing these healthy animals exposes the moral superficiality of triple-R efforts. If we were truly concerned about animals and genuinely believed that what we are doing is a "necessary *evil*," we would come out with better ideas than euthanizing scientifically "useless," healthy rodents.

"Compensating" animals sounds peculiar, and in today's climate is an oddity, but it does merit reflection. Interspecies compensation is probably the wrong term, as the experimented animal is not the animal that benefits. But there are three important moral gains if research institutions provided funds for saving, say, three animals for each animal that they kill. First, the overall outcome will be better for animals. Second, the act of compensation will encapsulate a financially backed recognition of the immoral conduct being done (or minimally, some accountability for the fact that animals are harmed so as to benefit humans). Third, such compensation enables a research scientist, at the end of his work day, to know that with regard to animals as such, his work has contributed to saving many of them, not just promoting their death. This last gain—the linkage between scientists in particular and animal welfare—is complex: on the one hand, society benefits from scientific work, and so it cannot be fair to scientists to dissociate between "science" and society when speaking of such "compensation." On the other hand, tying research to compensation is sensitive to the moral and psychological needs of the particular men and women who are actually involved in the killing. "Compensation" can take the institutional form of rehabilitation centers that begin by giving these animals a life, some life, after they have been used (rather than packaging them off to zoos as food—a not uncommon practice with survivors).

Such thoughts are obviously utopian. When animal exploitation for trivial human gain is so widespread and nonapologetic, one can only be apologetic about impractical remarks. The moral bottom line is clear: to be counted as a "morally justified immorality," as the above arguments claim, such experimentation has to meet weighty requirements that, when spelled out, demand a fundamental reform of current research practice. There is small hope that such will occur.[38]

PRACTICAL CONSEQUENCES

But do we really want to see laboratories shut down and all animal-based experimental research stopped? Do we wish to join hands with varieties of antiscientists that do not share a fundamental respect for the spirit of inquiry underlying research, that have never felt wonder or pride or delight at understanding the complexities that science unravels? Can we genuinely undertake the responsibility for actively stopping or slowing down the search for better medication that will cure us and our relatives (as well as our companion and farm animals) in years to come? Do we wish to risk trying out on ourselves new products and chemicals, doing away with in vivo screening? And what about the inconvenience of attacking the people with whom we have lunch in academic cafeterias, those to which some of us (me) are attached by family ties, and who bring respectability and funding to the institutions in which we work? Farmers were always easy targets for intellectuals concerned with the maltreatment of animals. Picking on the academic colleagues next door is much more awkward. Telling scientists that their work is immoral is presumptuous and antisocial, and telling them that their work can be done using alternatives requires the expertise that only scientist themselves have. Tom Regan urges scientists to look for alternative research models to those deployed today, adding that this is a first-rate scientific challenge. Regan's suggestion is consistent with the line taken by most antivivisectionists, who refuse to see the elimination of animal-based experimentation as an attack on science or product testing as such. But one can readily expect scientists who are genuinely driven by the desire to explore a particular phenomenon to be reluctant about spending years to locate means to explore the phenomenon instead. Devising controls on experiments and searching for alternatives, enforcing on reluctant scientists the use of models that they would rather not use—all this is not exciting or prestigious work.

Acknowledging such weighty pragmatic, social, and intellectual concerns cannot modify the conclusions of the previous discussion, and

---

[38] "Small" rather than no hope, since experimentation is susceptible to legislation, which is itself interesting because legislation preventing activities that promote less weighty human ends, e.g., recreational fishing, are today still unimaginable.

different practical implications can be derived from them. My own view regarding these implications (which need not be shared by others who accept my previous analysis) begins with a pessimistic prediction: animal research is not going to stop in the next decades (at least not due to moral claims). The reason for this pessimism is not merely that reform takes time—fully correcting human exploitation takes decades, possibly more—but that, in comparison with the large-scale killing of animals for much lighter reasons, animal-based research presents the strongest claim for using animals in exploitative ways. Animal experimentation is situated at the end of a moral continuum, in which steps like a large-scale banning of recreational fishing and moral vegetarianism morally precede the termination of vivisection. These lighter stages have not even begun on a social scale. Stopping animal research should morally and logically be the last stop on a long road, and the suspicion that some of those who oppose it have not undertaken personal measures of protest against less important reasons for animal exploitation suggests that nonmoral motives play a strong part in antivivisection sentiment.[39] Proresearch literature speculates that antiscience and antiestablishment feelings animate antivivisectionist protest, and this may explain why scientists and their laboratories have been attacked in various places throughout the world, but farmers and abattoir owners remain outside the pale of the more violent sides of liberationist action. I am obviously not advocating bombing factory-farms to create consistency within the pro-animal movement. But the anomaly of making scientists rather than your next-door, meat-consuming family the prime targets—your average meat-consuming neighbor commissions the killing of many more animals than does your average experimental scientist, and she is doing so for far less

---

[39] Nicoll and Russell ("A Darwinian View," 166) rely on a demographic breakdown of participants in the "March for Animals" held on 1990 in Washington, DC. The research they draw from was conducted by W. Jamison and W. Lunch and published in *Science, Technology, and Human Values* 17 (4) (1992): 438–58. Nicoll and Russell focus on the fact that 80 percent of the protesters did not have children, which leads them to the bizarre speculation that antivivisectionists are "adaptively unfit" from an evolutionary perspective. As a parent of three children, I fear that I belong to the remaining anomalous 20 percent, for whom Nicoll and Russell probably reserve an even more degrading explanation. Be that as it may, I wish to note a different finding in the data they present. According to Jamison and Lunch's demographic data, only 78 percent of those opposed to experiments were either vegan or vegetarian. The fact that one of every five protesters was not willing to compromise his or her diet but was attempting to change someone else's medication strikes me as strange. It may be the case that some of those opposed to animal experimentation were only protesting against usage of higher animals, or that the remaining 22 percent were protesting because of prudential arguments against the benefits of such experiments. But I fear that there may also be nonmoral factors at play. Rudacille's book, *The Scalpel and the Butterfly*, is a fascinating exploration of the nonmoral sentiments that underlie antivivisectionist thought.

reason—indicates complex motivation in antivivisection thought, which does not necessarily cohere with the narrowly moral underpinnings of pro-animal protest. If social policy follows moral soundness, abattoirs should be shut down before laboratories.

To anticipate objections to what I have just said, I am not envisaging moral progress as a neatly structured movement, flowing logically from one step to the next. Nor am I deflating my previous attempts at refuting the justifications of research, or playing into the hands of supporters of research by allowing them to say that we should morally wait until society at large endorses moral vegetarianism. I am also, I believe, not misperceiving the strategic goal of beginning with the hardest case for animal liberation, enlisting the prestige of science into the battle over animal reform, or belittling the killing of more than forty million animals a year. I am instead endorsing what appears to me to be a viable strategic stance that acknowledges that it would take a long time for society to unshackle itself from present exploitative practices. The primary strategic focus of liberation should at present be banning killing and exploitation for trivial ends. Managing that, in this century, would in itself be a tremendous achievement for liberationists. The research community can even be enlisted to promote such a goal rather than being alienated from it, because it is precisely researchers' insistence on the worthiness of their causes for sacrificing animals that should lead them to condemn so many unworthy reasons for killing animals. Quadruple-R thinking (including rehabilitation) can pave the way to recognizing that "replacement" not only takes place in the laboratory but relates to one's nutrition as well.

Strategic prudence should not be confused with moral analysis. I strived to show why experiments cannot be morally excused. But, at least for me, what follows from such a result is not a tooth-and-nail battle aimed at the ceasing of all vivisection. It is seldom realized that consistently fighting such a battle could demand paying a saintly personal price, since it may require giving up on the benefits of past and future animal research (avoiding various vaccines, open-heart surgery, most drugs, numerous—if not all—household chemicals). Otherwise, one's consumption of such goods is to benefit from a wrong.[40] Walking down the antivivisection road

---

[40] I am not claiming that antivivisectionists are committed to refraining from medication. One could consistently benefit from a wrong and at the same time demand that it stop. Too many of our institutions, political arrangements, economic circumstances, and so forth implicate us in benefiting from some wrong. The morally correct response to this realization is not disconnection from the past wrong, but trying to redress it, compensate the victims (when possible), or change things so that it is not reiterated on new victims. Yet while this point holds on the level of collective morality, the personal dimension of consuming products that rely on what Godlovitch calls "nasty knowledge" may be different. On the moral status of consumption predicated on wrong action, see the previous

consistently may then substantially diminish the scope of liberationism by turning it into an unlivable mode of protest, thus damaging animals in the long run. The time may come when animal-using laboratories will become proper targets for change. That time is not here yet.

This does not mean that laboratories should not be severely monitored. Indeed, pro-animalists should work assiduously to establish and enforce ethical regulations on research, create substantial fund allocations to alternatives, promote routine work with now-available international data banks presenting updated information on validated alternatives, as well as improve these data banks.[41] As for more robust forms of protest, we are perhaps ready for blanket banning of experimentation on some of the higher species and some variants of basic research.[42] We may be ready to eliminate all teaching-related killing of animals, using the alternatives that are already available for these.[43] We are beginning to ban the testing of some products on animals (cosmetics and tobacco). But we are not ready for anything more ambitious. If some think that such remarks are defeatist, so be it. Stopping all animal experimentation is a morally correct objective, but, for the time being, aim lower.

---

chapter. For the specific moral status of consumption that presupposes knowledge derived immorally, see S. Godlovitch, "Forbidding Nasty Knowledge: On the Use of Ill-gotten Information," *Journal of Applied Philosophy* 14 (1) (1997): 1–18.

[41] One problem here is that there are too many data banks that are themselves uncoordinated, and so information found in one need not be accessible in another. Although these databases are usually free, this lack of overlap necessitates multiple searches and mastering the particularities of too many search engines. The John Hopkins-based ALTWEB provides links and explanations regarding the ones that exist (http://altweb.jhsph.edu) and can thus provide an easy starting point. The German ZEBET–Centre for Documentation and Evaluation of Alternatives to Animal Experiments has an online searchable database on alternatives (http://www. bgvv.de/cd/1591) that is unique in providing assessments of the status of given alternatives as well as explanation of their nature and possible application. The ZEBET site thus is not merely a search engine, but produces its own overview of a given alternative (in August 2005 the database had 118 such assessments, adding a new one at the rate of one review per month). ECVAM has both an old database and a new one, DB-ALM (http://ecvam.jrc.it). ECVAM deals only with alternatives to toxicity tests. The absolute number of validated alternatives that one actually finds on these engines is disappointingly small (the ECVAM database, for example, has less than ten validated alternatives). Yet, as William Stokes of ICCVAM pointed out to me, this small number is misleading since some of the existing validated alternatives may be extremely important and effective in terms of the actual number of affected animals.

[42] The relevant argument is made in Wise, *Rattling the Cage*.

[43] The European Resource Centre Alternatives in Higher Education (EURCA, http://www.eurca.org) and the Norwegian Reference Centre for Laboratory Animal Science database (NORINA, http://www.norinadatabase.org) are two important resources for information on alternatives in education. For literature on such alternatives, see also Nick Jukes and Mihnea Chiuia, *From Guinea Pig to Computer Mouse: Alternative Methods for a Progressive, Humane Education* (Leicester, England: InterNICHE, 2003).

At the same time, I am not claiming that we can dispense with the opposition to research. I see two valid practical routes for opposition: the first is fighting to ban all experiments. The second is less dramatic and exciting yet might well be a more effective intervention on behalf of animals: join hands with the worldwide attempt to reduce the number of animal experiments, to diminish animal pain in experiments that are carried out, and to rehabilitate animals that survive nonterminal experiments. These two options seem to be mutually exclusive: advancing the second (e.g., by participating in an ethical committee) implies (rightly or wrongly) acceptance of the premises that some experiments need to be conducted, and this contradicts the assumption that all animal experiments are morally wrong, the assumption animating the first option of actively fighting to stop all experiments. Moreover, by lending one's name as a pro-animal activist to the authorization of experiments, one appears to be, in effect, publicly providing a moral stamp of approval to a practice that one opposes.

Both options have proven to be effective in different ways: categorical consumer bans have been partly responsible for the seventh amendment of the European Union Cosmetics Directive, which prohibits any animal-based safety testing of cosmetics from 2009 on (such products already cannot be tested on animals in Germany). They have also prompted cosmetic companies to fund research into alternative product testing. Categorical and uncompromising student protests have also made a difference. One example is the University of Marburg, Germany, in which such protests managed to stop the use of animals as part of physiology courses.[44] Moreover, without vehement and systematic opposition to animal experiments, triple-R policies would not have been endorsed to begin with.

On the other hand (in terms of effectiveness), work done on validating alternatives has succeeded in eliminating some experiments and techniques that involved death or severe pain to numerous animals. A notable example is the Murine Local Lymph Node Assay, which has dramatically reduced the number of guinea pigs used as part of a particular test. Efforts to replace LD 50 toxicity testing (determining toxicity levels by examining exposure level that kills 50 percent of the animals) by the revised up-and-down Procedure for Determining Acute Oral Toxicity are also important in attempts to practically and substantially change things for the better. The work done on devising humane endpoints for experiments (early biomarkers such as weight loss or urinary change that can indicate toxicity and that the experiment can be terminated without waiting for

---

[44] The story and outcome of this struggle are given in Jukes and Chiuia, *From Guinea Pig to Computer Mouse.*

acute toxicity signs such as severe pain or death) is likewise a practical attempt to reduce pain. The numerous individuals and organizations that are industriously devoted to bringing about these changes (the European ECVAM, the U.S. ICCVAM, the German ZEBET, or the Dutch NCA as well as the animal-welfare organizations that partly back the search for alternatives) are surely effectively diminishing unnecessary pain and death for many animals.

So should a believer in the immorality of experiments oppose animal-based research or chip in and join the international effort to reduce, refine, and replace some experiments? Logically, these are not mutually excluding strategies: one can protest against animal experiments as such, yet as long as that goal cannot be achieved, energetically participate in four-R initiatives, or in promoting the implementation of these once they are validated. Psychologically, however, such reconciliation might prove more difficult to maintain in one of the more important spheres of possible action: ethical committees. Ironically, if one actually attains some institutional power by being invited to serve on such a committee, one is likely to be asked to authorize and actively promote projects that one deeply objects to (e.g., projects that incorporate humane endpoints that reduce suffering but in effect mean that the animal is euthanized earlier). Even if there is no moral or logical contradiction between service on such a committee and a rejection of the moral validity of animal experimentation, it seems to me that trying to reconcile both agendas in practice can be a taxing task indeed for a liberationist. Should liberationists serve on such committees, contributing their distinct impact to the considerations being factored in (some countries, such as Sweden, incorporate animal-welfare advocates as part of the formal makeup of their committees)? I do not have a decisive answer here. But given my pessimistic outlook on the slim prospects for fundamental change, I think that they should. In-house opposition and screening by the people who speak for animal reform not only would effectively help animals, but would foster the kind of dialogue that is often lacking here and can have long lasting consequences. Transforming animal-based education, research, and product testing will take time and the work of several generations. Rather than adopting the stance of moral purity and avoiding such work and the hard compromises it demands, I would be happier to know that liberationists are an integrated part in this endeavor. I ask for their participation, and it need not be enthusiastic.

PART III

Using

Chapter 5

USE OR EXPLOITATION?

THIS SECTION OF THE BOOK examines practices that do not involve killing nonhuman animals. The status of animals that live their lives in zoos or farms, or function as companion animals (pets) or therapy animals, is debated among liberationists. Some perceive each of these practices as further manifestations of speciesist culture that ought to be eradicated in a just world. Other liberationists accept some but not all of these practices. Aside from liberationists, determining the moral status of these practices is important, not merely because it specifies and rationalizes the envisaged reform being proposed, but also because it affects numerous individuals who are personally involved in such practices and who regard themselves as deeply attached to the animals with which they interact. Pet owners are sometimes morally concerned about actions like limiting their pet's freedom, or subjecting the animal to invasive procedures that curtail its reproductive capacity. Practitioners of animal-assisted therapy are themselves often animal lovers who worry about the morality (or lack of it) of such uses of the animals for which they deeply care. Moral vegetarians doubt that their personal protest is insufficient, and that veganism is the more consistent moral decision.

Morally assessing such practices is an outcropping of the distinction between use and exploitation. If such a distinction is impossible to draw, than virtually all animal-related practices should disappear in a just world. Antipet liberationists and some moral vegans are in effect endorsing this categorical position. On the other hand, if exploitation can be set apart from use, than liberationism proves to be a more flexible position that can accommodate some animal-related practices while objecting to others. The issue here is sometimes entangled by the deployment of "instrumentality" and avoiding "instrumentalizing" others, an idea that is repeatedly invoked yet difficult to unpack clearly, even in human contexts. We routinely use our friends and relatives for emotional or physical support. We use other people for their abilities, knowledge, and work power, and such give-and-take relations are legitimate. The relevant moral distinction is accordingly *not* the one between instrumentalization and noninstrumentalization, but the one between use and exploitation. Kant was unhelpful regarding this, holding that whereas in some contexts it is permissible to treat another person as a means, it is immoral to perceive another person *merely* as a means. This position is notoriously vague, since it appeals to private motivations that are easily given to manipulation and rationalization. People can (and do) exploit others while commending themselves for negligible concessions that they make for the benefit of the exploited party.

Fortunately, the distinction between use and exploitation is not hard to draw. X uses Y when he perceives Y as a means of furthering his own financial (or other) well-being. This turns into exploitation when X is willing to act in a way that is substantially detrimental to Y's own well-being in order to further his own. By "substantial" I mean that the action predictably carries consequences such as shortening Y's life, damaging his health, limiting his freedom, abusing what he is (e.g., some forms of prostitution), systematically thwarting his potential (e.g., child labor), or subjecting him to pain or to a strongly undesired life (e.g., demanding inhuman workloads and thus creating human-slavery). Exploitation usually also suggests lack of consent by the exploited party (or a consent that is predicated on a highly limited choice or on choosing among impossible alternatives). Exploitation is also mostly related to the existence of unequal power relations or some dependency relations between the parties, favoring the exploiting party in an institutional and systematic way.

To know for certain that he is not exploiting Y, merely using him, X must be in a relationship such that he is repeatedly making choices that substantively further Y's welfare even when in conflict with X's own prudential motives. This need not mean that X is to become irrational or altruistic. It merely suggests how a person can actually verify that she is not involved in an exploitative relationship. I believe that people can legitimately fall short of this ideal. That is, they can be uncertain as to whether or not a particular relationship that they have is exploitative. Give-and-take relations can be vague in this sense. For example, immigrants in well-off countries sometimes offer to overwork themselves to provide for the families in their home country. Fantasizing about global justice is a commendable thought-experiment, but it does not help one when compelled to choose between cooperating with such requests by hiring these immigrants or not. One does not always know. And provided that one does not knowingly participate in or cooperate with clearcut exploitative relations, I believe that it is morally permissible to have relations over which one has some misgivings.

How can one tell whether one is in a "clear-cut" exploitative relationship? Generally, you are clearly exploiting someone if your relationship predictably benefits you and harms the person involved. This holds for human as well as nonhuman animals (though some will vindicate exploitation in relation to the latter but not the former). More specifically and in light of the various characterizations of exploitative relationships mentioned above, the criteria include both a quantitative and a qualitative specification: relationships become more exploitative if they share more of the characteristics spelled out above (this is the "quantitative" answer). At the same time, a relationship can manifest only one of the characteristics mentioned above in some substantial way and be clearly exploitative (the "qualitative" answer). These differentiating characteristics are applicable to our relations with nonhuman animals too. If, for example, I provide an entity with a comfortable life in which it is not abused in any way, yet aim to kill it when it is very young, the relationship is clearly exploitative. If, on the other hand, I intend to terminate the entity's life only if it becomes old or incurably ill, I am not exploiting it, even if I would not act in the same way with regard to a human being. This is why relationships between pet and owner can be nonexploitative (although they might constitute use), and why the same cannot be said concerning the lamb industry. I am not claiming that distinguishing between use and exploitation is always simple. Indeed, animal ethics provides many vague cases (free roaming, debeaked hens, for instance). But the considerations that could lead us to determine the status of such cases are not mysterious, and often indicate decisive answers.[1]

A critic might object to my moving from human to nonhuman contexts. The objection will not be against my characterization of exploitation as such but will focus on its moral significance. Some might try to defend the idea that exploitation is wrong only when it applies to humans. This position need not be coupled with the Cartesian or Kantian categorical denial of moral considerability to animals that was rejected earlier in this book. The critic will here follow what appears to be the consensus in many countries: animals are entitled to some moral considerability (and this basically means that cruelty to animals ought to be prevented). Yet nothing stands in the way of exploiting animals for all kinds of purposes. The response to this argument ("But if it is wrong to be cruel to an entity, how can it be right to exploit it?") will be dismissed by adopting a "degrees" view of moral considerability: animals have some degree of moral considerability (which justifies preventing abuse of them), but not enough to prohibit exploiting them.

Yet the degrees view cannot be accepted. Apart from questions about its validity as a thesis, the morally relevant properties that generate the prohibition on cruelty—the animal's capacity to suffer as well as its

[1] I am focusing on elements that are shared in exploitation of humans and nonhumans. There are additional elements that are unique to the exploitation of humans (e.g., disrespect for a person's actual or potential autonomy, maintaining a humiliating relationship, blocking information, systematically lying). Such may figure as elements that constitute some form of exploitative relationships when applied to humans but have no such significance when ascribed to nonhuman animals.

possession of an interest/desire not to be subjected to some actions—are shared by humans too. In the case of humans, it is partly these properties that underlie the condemnation of exploiting them. It would therefore appear mysterious why—if one is willing to admit these properties into an analysis (and condemnation) of one kind of conduct—one dismisses these very same properties when analyzing another entity. If, for example, one opposes cruelty to animals because their suffering is morally relevant (and not just because cruelty is reprehensible as such), one is obligated to avoid actions that induce such suffering.

What this means, morally, is that when pursuing human interests requires animal suffering, we cannot simply permit these interests to annul our obligation to avoid creating suffering. We are morally required to devise alternatives to these conflicts of interests. Many (not all) human-animal conflicts of interests can be finessed, meaning that it is possible to meet the human need in a substantial—though sometimes not maximal—way, without compromising the well-being of animals. Recognizing this makes it possible to avoid a host of second-order questions regarding the relative importance of human interests, as well as the plausibility (or lack of it) of mobilizing this import to thwart particular animal interests. One does not have to exploit animals in order to obtain eggs or milk, for example. The same applies to animal-assisted therapy: there are numerous effective modes of therapy that do not exploit animals, so there is no reason to institutionalize modes that do.

The following chapters implement the use/exploitation distinction for three use-related practices. I will argue that some animal-related institutionalized activities constitute merely use and can be morally vindicated and preserved given reform. Others cannot be justified and must be abolished.

Chapter 6

CULINARY USE

VEGANS CHARGE MORAL VEGETARIANS with inconsistency: if eating animals is a participation in a wrong practice, consuming egg and dairy products is likewise wrong because it constitutes cooperation with systematic exploitation.[1] Vegans say that even the more humane parts of the contemporary dairy and egg industry rely on immoral practices, and that therefore moral vegetarianism is too small a step in the right direction. According to vegans, moral vegetarians have conceded that animals are not means; that human pleasure cannot override animal suffering and death; that some industries ought to be banned; and that all this carries practical implications regarding their own actions. Yet according to vegans, vegetarians disingenuously stop short of a full realization of what speciesist culture involves and what living a moral life in such an environment requires. Moral vegans distinguish themselves from moral vegetarians in accepting the practical prescriptions of altogether avoiding benefiting from animal exploitation, not just of avoiding benefiting from the killing. Vegans take the killing to be merely one aspect of the systematic exploitation of animals.

If it is wrong to kill an entity of a particular kind, it is probably wrong to exploit it. And if it is wrong to benefit from the entity killed, it seems wrong to benefit from that entity being exploited. The moral logic of veganism appears sound. The viability of moral vegetarianism depends on the ability to establish a meaningful difference between animal-derived "products" that vegetarians boycott and those that they can legitimately consume. Moral vegetarians agree that the egg and dairy industry has to be radically reformed. The difference between vegans and vegetarians does not then relate to the premise that exploitation exists, but to the practical conclusion drawn from the premise: some moral vegans say that no production of egg and dairy can be nonexploitative (call these "vegans"), while others hold to a more provisional position: *given* that animals are heavily exploited in such industries, one's hopes for reform are beside the moral point (call these "tentative vegans"). Tentative

---

[1] The labels "vegan" and "vegetarian" in this chapter, apply only to moral vegans and moral vegetarians where the distinguishing feature between these is consumption of ovo-lacto products (sometimes the ban extends to honey). I will ignore vegans and vegetarians for whom these are merely dietary choices that relate to healthy living.

vegans agree that egg and dairy products can be produced without exploitation. Yet they cannot see how it may be justified to cooperate with such practices as a consumer given their present immoral nature.

Moral vegetarians will probably purchase egg and dairy products from sources that boast of morally progressive breeding conditions (morally progressive steps obviously do not constitute morally *acceptable* conditions). Buying products from manufacturers that maintain free-roaming animals is surely a step forward.[2] But vegans and vegetarians will agree that it is not enough. The space allowed for captive animals is only one of many features that constitute the exploitative nature of such breeding. It is easier for a manufacturer to meet the requirement for space than, say, avoiding practices that reduce the animals into overworked, living factories that "manufacture" much more than they would have done naturally. Free-roaming laying hens are exploited if they are killed when they become "unproductive" or if the breeding facility kills day-old unproductive male chicks while allowing their sisters to free-range (or if it obtains its hens from hatching facilities that kill male chicks). Debeaking, a painful procedure that is widely practiced with regard to non-free-roaming as well as free-roaming hens (at least where I live, the free-roaming hens are routinely debeaked), also spoils the image of "free-roaming" animals as creatures that live their lives without painful intervention by humans motivated by financial gain. Should vegetarians cooperate with an industry that, even at its moral best, employs standards that abuse animals?

Right or wrong, the vegan-vegetarian debate concerns a very small group of philosophers. More are interested in the internal coherence of moral vegetarianism. Yet pro-animal authors many times opt to leave vague the specific practical prescriptions that their work implies. The reason for this openness is that given the present negligible impact of pro-animal protest, it seems strategically wise not to quibble over the precise contours of the objective. Animals gain more from those that write on their behalf if these do not try to overzealously embarrass people who are willing to make only partial concessions to the pro-animal cause. Vagueness may be strategically wise, but it carries a price as one is upholding an ideal that is not fully explained. Apart from deciding whether veganism or vegetarianism is the more persuasive opposition to

---

[2] John Webster challenges this claim. He argues that free-roaming breeding is ideal only for a very small number of hens, not in commercial units. His evidence is that about half of the birds in commercial free-roaming units elect not to leave the house (*Animal Welfare*, 158). Webster's evidence does not support his conclusion: even if birds opt to stay in, that does not imply that such breeding is as bad as battery cages. But I agree with Webster that free-roaming facilities will probably not be the last word should poultry husbandry be reformed.

current animal-related practice, this chapter also explores the justification of the way by which vegetarians draw the limits of their protest. I will argue that vegetarianism is a morally superior regulative ideal and a more effective form of protest compared to veganism. I begin by arguing against veganism. I shall then turn to tentative veganism.

VEGANISM

Pro-animal action partly depends on how one envisages ideal relations between humans and nonhumans. "Stop all coercion and violence"— such is the most extreme pro-animal position imaginable. According to this hands-off position, usage and killing of whatever kind are to stop. Companion animals are also out, since keeping them involves limiting their movement and may detrimentally affect other wild animals. Regulative beliefs of this kind will surely prescribe moral veganism. A less extreme position allows pets in the regulative ideal but bans raising animals for meat, milk, and eggs regardless of the conditions in which this is done. This too implies moral veganism. A second notch down is the ideal that regulates moral vegetarianism: here animals are never killed for their flesh, but they are maintained as pets, or for eggs and milk. Moral vegetarianism is consistent with eating animals that die on their own (scavenging) or using their hides after they die. Euthanasia is also practiced and is considered justified so long as it is done for the animal's own welfare, rather than for the purpose of using its body later. I will now argue that moral veganism of both kinds above is a bad ideal both for humans and for animals. To do so I intend to consider companion animals first, since *if* our attitude toward them can be morally vindicated, such can function as a regulative ideal for other human-animal relations.

Well-kept pets are a source of joy to their owners, live a much better life than they would have lived in the wild, and, as far as I can tell, pay a small price for such conditions.[3] A petless world is bad for cats and dogs, an overwhelming number of which would not survive out of human care. It is a bad world for humans, since they lose an important source of happiness, and it is bad for the animal welfare cause, since strong relations with pets prompt many people to think morally about animals. Acts against the pet's will can be condemned as coercive only if we

---

[3] I fail to see anything demeaning about the word "pet," nor am I clear whether "demeaning" or "humiliating" an animal is even possible rather than an anthropocentric imposition. I shall use "pet" and "companion animal" interchangeably. For an attempt to analyze the category of a pet, see Gary Varner's "Pets, Companion Animals, and Domesticated Partners," in *Ethics for Everyday*, ed. David Benatar, 450–75 (Boston: McGraw-Hill, 2002).

anthropomorphicize such animals into autonomous individuals. But it seems to me that a more adequate organizing moral framework through which pets are to be understood is quasi-paternalistic: the status of pets resembles that of children, though unlike children, who enter a temporary paternalistic relation with a guardian, pets remain in a permanent paternalistic relationship. The relationship is not fully paternalistic, since, unlike with children, one is not merely a guardian acting with only their interests in mind but is also acting with the interest of preserving the relationship as such. Many morally problematic, invasive owner actions, such as limiting movement, sterilizing, or declawing, are conceptualized (and sometimes justified) in this light. One is sometimes acting on behalf of the animal (a neutered cat lives longer), but one is also acting on behalf of the relationship: one cannot, for example, keep a cat and its litter, or one cannot maintain one's cat and one's baby when the former is not declawed and the latter develops a habit of pulling hairy things. Justified owner actions with regard to pets are thus either an action directly on behalf of the pet or an action in the interest of maintaining the relationship between owner and pet, a relationship that is itself an overall good for the pet. This obviously does not determine *which* action can legitimately be perceived as justified in order to maintain the relationship (e.g., cutting the vocal cords of a parrot or a dog because it disturbs its owner is immoral, even if it does benefit the relationship by enabling the animal to continue living with its owner). And the question of which invasive actions are justified for the sake of the owner-pet relationship is the most important question within small animal veterinary ethics.

The most reasonable pro-animal answer to this question is utilitarian: examining overall utility for animals.[4] Some invasive actions merely benefit the pet (e.g., vaccination). Some benefit the owner and cause pain and possible complications to the pet without benefiting the animal (e.g., tail docking and ear cropping). Some involve loss to the pet, which it need not necessarily experience as a loss (spaying, neutering). Given a paternalistic framework, the first kind are unproblematically moral. The second are unproblematically immoral. The moral status of the third kind is complex: humans would not be spayed and neutered even if such provided them with longer lives, and so longevity does not trump the loss of sexual and procreative capacities. On the other hand, conceiving of human-human action solely through paternalistic terms is in itself

---

[4] I am not a utilitarian, and I do not consider the following endorsement of a utilitarian consideration in evaluating competing courses of action in one domain of moral life to necessitate adopting a utilitarian position. My remarks above should trouble only those who oppose any use of utilitarian considerations.

already immoral. Moreover, unlike pets, the idea that some actions are justified morally since they enable the owner-pet relationship to exist is also foreign to human-human morality.

Unlike human children, who would—hypothetically—grow up and could decide for themselves whether they wish to lose their sexual abilities so as to live longer, companion animals can never attain such autonomy. We make the decision for them. Is it the right decision? I think that it is, for four reasons that concern the particular pet's welfare as well as the welfare of other pets: first, as said, such actions promote the pet's own longevity. Second, when one avoids anthropocentric dismay at the loss of sexual or procreative capacities, no evidence suggests that the pet conceives of its postoperative state as a loss (unlike us, cats and dogs have no consistent sex drive, and once heating cycles are not created, there is no evidence that this loss is experienced as undesirable). Third, many people will not have pets if this implies undertaking responsibility for many potential offspring. Fourth, without spaying and neutering, we will have many more abandoned animals that lead miserable lives, spread contagious diseases among their species and others, and ultimately, may have to be killed in shelters.

Invasive actions that benefit the pet are justified through a paternalistic framework or through assuming that the owner-pet relationship is valuable and beneficial for pets. Muting a parrot or a dog (unlike parrots, dogs are known to be muted in some countries), tail docking, or ear trimming cannot obviously be excused through such means. Euthanizing pets is usually conceptualized as an action on their behalf, and when this is the case, the action is justified.[5] Declawing is problematic: owners that ask for such a procedure for their cats many times will not keep their animals otherwise. Such declawing can then benefit the pet. But sometimes the request for the (painful) procedure stems from owner irresponsibility, not realizing the implication of having a pet of a specific kind. If the person asking for the procedure does so because Kitty destroys her beloved sofa, there is a sense in which she should have foreseen this when she undertook responsibility for a cat.[6] Unlike spaying or neutering, here Kitty

---

[5] Sometimes this conceptualization resembles a rationalization, and even an institutional one, like the case of large-scale euthanizing of stray or abandoned companion animals in animal shelters. For an analysis of the moral viability of this often ignored lacuna in animal ethics, see Lee Anne Fennell, "Killing with Kindness: An Inquiry into the Routinized Destruction of Companion Animals," in *Between the Species*, 3 (web-journal), 2003.

[6] On moral responsibility to companion animals, see Keith Burgess-Jackson, "Doing Right by Our Animal Companions," *Journal of Ethics* 2 (1998): 159–85. Gary Varner ("Pets") surveys other accounts of moral responsibility to pets (by Rollin and DeGrazia). Varner, too, is justifying pet keeping through appealing to the overall utility for animals.

does not gain anything by the procedure. And so there is reason for a veterinarian not to cooperate with this request. In an ideal world, no owner who cares that much for her sofa will take in a cat. The veterinarian ought to urge the owner to withdraw her request. If, however, the owner insists and there is a strong possibility that the cat will be abandoned if the procedure is not conducted, it is overall better for the cat to be declawed, and so the veterinarian should perform the procedure. The overall utility of simply outlawing declawing for animals (as is the case in San Francisco, where such legislation seems very close) is thus unclear. For the same utilitarian considerations, maiming animals in order to have them as pets, or actions that violate what they are (wing trimming in birds, caging birds), have nothing to do with the animal's own welfare. As far as I can tell, such actions do seem to be a loss to the animal, and they do seem to be experienced as such. Unlike cats, dogs, and horses, birds in the wild lead better lives than caged ones. Caging a bird appears to me to be in the same category as socially isolating a dog or a chimpanzee: some distortion of what that animal is ("distortion" in the sense of systematically frustrating some constitutive need in a way that seems to be experienced as such). The greater safety that they gain does not counterbalance the losses birds like parrots pay for sharing their lives with humans. The same argument applies to keeping wild animals as pets: most are better off in the wild.

Pets can of course be maltreated, and veterinarians ought not be idealized, since financial incentives sometimes turn them into tools that satisfy any whim an owner may express. Nor do I mean to shortcut the problematic nature of disconnecting animals from members of their own species. Some pets are loners (cats); others learn to treat humans as their pack (dogs). Disconnection, in such cases, does not appear problematic. The situation with regard to simian helpers of disabled humans is less clear. Pro-animal utopia will probably involve some reform of pet husbandry, training, and medicine. But such reform will not be radical. Pets benefit from leading lives with humans, and the price they pay is small in comparison. Companion animal husbandry looks like a reasonable exchange: pets do lose through this relationship, but they get to lead safe and comfortable lives, and they die when they are old or sick. The alternative of a petless world does not strike me as morally superior or as overall better for animals.

Here, then, is a model of human-animal relationships that, although we call all the shots (saying what seems "reasonable," "acceptable," "plausible exchange," etc.), is morally justified on utilitarian grounds; a model in which the overall good is determined in relation to all the entities concerned, even when it does prescribe invasive actions and curtailing the animal's freedom.

Vegan Utopia

Companion animals show that human-animal relations need not be exploitative. Cows, sheep, and hens are not pets, and people have them for different reasons from those that lead them to take in cats and dogs. People wish to use farm animals. Use need not be exploitation, and if our relations with pets present a nonexploitative regulative ideal, the ability to maintain nonexploitative relationships with farm animals depends, in part, on the ability to import elements from our relations with pets into the world of farm-animal husbandry.

Before asking how such an ideal can be worked out, I need to specify what is bad about the vegan alternative. If eggs and milk cannot be had without exploitation, a pro-animal ideal state means that laying hens and cows will either disappear or be maintained in small numbers in specially created reserves. Quantitatively, such a world is bad for these animals since less of them would exist. The argument is familiar, but it has usually been made by meat-eaters against vegetarians, not by vegetarians against vegans. And so I need to say why considerations of the value of a lived life can be legitimately employed by vegetarians in this dispute.[7] Philosophers will also worry about the plausibility of arguing from the projected benefits of nonexistent entities: in what sense can a world that does not include a particular cow be bad for "it" (for the nonexistent cow) relative to a world in which "it" will exist? Doubtful too is the underlying assumption that more lives are better than few. After all, the quantitative argument against veganism is not that vegetarianism will enable a species to remain in existence (vegan utopia could preserve some farm animals), but that more members of that species will exist. And this emphasis on more-is-better is suspect.

Here are my reasons against these dismissals. Begin with the projected benefits of nonexistent entities. Many philosophers say that such moves are meaningless and reject the viability of a standpoint of a yet nonexistent entity that gains or loses. Ruling out such a standpoint is surely correct, but note that it does not follow that judgments regarding projected benefits of nonexistent entities are meaningless (e.g., when we speak about our obligation to future generations). When we say that a yet nonexistent entity gains by our actions—e.g., claiming that future generations benefit or are harmed by particular ecological steps that are undertaken now; or

---

[7] Leahy, Scruton, and Hare have used this argument in the past against vegetarians. In chapter 3 I argued at length against this claim as a justification of meat eating. Here I shall claim that it is a plausible move against veganism. I shall also say why I think one can consistently reject this argument as a justification of eating meat, and accept it as an argument against veganism.

leaving an inheritance to a yet unborn grandchild; or feeling gratitude to a parent for "giving us life"—we do not assume an *already existing* perspective of these future generations, or future grandchildren, or rely on a comparison with some "preexisting us" that has benefited by receiving the gift of life. Such statements do not exemplify meaningless metaphysical blunder, because they are predicated on a conditional projection: a yet nonexistent entity, *if* it existed, would benefit or lose through a present action. The conditional nature of the judgment is why I cannot harm an entity by not bringing it into the world (I do not harm another future child of mine by not bringing it into the world). Such entities can be harmed neither now nor in the future since they do not and will not exist. At the same time, such entities would benefit should I bring them into the world and secure good living conditions for them. I can also harm them, should I bring them into some kinds of life. I am claiming, then, that there is an important temporal dissymmetry between harming/benefiting and some other actions, say, hugging: while I can only hug now an existing person, I can harm or benefit now a nonexistent person, should that person exist in the future. The lack of a specific subject to a relational predicate does not make such statements meaningless, since the relation to a subject is established obliquely: "benefiting"/"harming" target a nonspecified individual that will gain or lose by a certain course of action. Only in hindsight can this statement gain a specified and well-defined referent. But it is perfectly meaningful prior to the instantiation stage. It is thus consistent to claim that a vegan utopia will not harm the farm animals that will not exist, but a vegetarian utopia will be a benefit to these, yet unborn ones. My comparative judgment that the vegetarian utopia is better than the vegan one does not, then, rely on the present perspective of the nonexistent animals, but on the future ones who will be "grateful" to discover that vegetarians rather than vegans won the day (we are, recall, discussing perfect worlds).

While this argument convinces me, I have encountered enough opposition to it to persuade me that some would regard it as a non sequitur.[8]

---

[8] First objection: the argument still refers to nonexistent entities, and these, by definition, cannot be benefited by bringing "them" into existence. Second objection: the argument shows that if a future being X will exist anyway, actions done now can benefit it—not that bringing it into existence benefits it. I have nothing much to add to what I have said above regarding the first objection. People can and do refer to future children that they plan to have, for example, planning names and establishing savings plans that would benefit them, without those children existing yet. I see no metaphysical confusion in such talk. Regarding the second, I say that if obtaining some future goods benefits an entity, then the condition for obtaining goods in the first place (existence) is also a good, so long as the future life is not considered as undesirable as such. This reasoning does not imply that existence is a property (should one desire to avoid that implication). It may be the case that "benefiting" is the wrong term to deploy in such a case, and that one may need to use different concepts. But devising a different terminology would not modify the moral point.

And so I shall add a nonmetaphysical consideration that supports the same conclusion. Since vegans may agree that the vegetarian may be able to provide farm animals with qualitatively good lives, promoting a course of action that would radically diminish the number of such lives is dubious. One need not be a utilitarian to perceive diverse lived experiences as themselves valuable and meriting respect. This does not entail an obligation to produce more lives or generate more species than those we currently have (the recognition of the value of distinct and diverse human lives does not, for example, imply that one is committed to creating more of them). Yet preserving diversity and a large species, if it already exists, seems on the face of it a morally superior goal in comparison to the virtual elimination of such beings. Loving cows, sheep, and hens into extinction is less plausible when set against the alternative of preserving those animals by allowing them to coexist with humans when they can be provided with qualitatively good lives.

Vegans will argue that a vegan utopia is still an overall good because it will reduce the number of lives that should not be lived. This was always the argument made against advocates of meat eating, who taunted vegetarians by saying that should vegetarianism win the day, fewer animals would exist, ergo, eating meat is an overall good for animals. The vegetarian counterargument (we saw) is that appealing to quantity is never enough, as life's value is not exhausted by its worth in relation to the living entity itself, and relates too to determining whether such a life should be lived (vegetarians thus do not subscribe to the more-is-better claim). But if mere existence is not enough for vegans or for vegetarians, why accept the vegetarian claim that their alternative is better for animals than the vegan one?

The question whether some lives should be lived can itself be partly determined by qualitative aspects: a life of perpetual torture or exploitation should not be lived if such can be prevented in advance. But like the quantitative dimension (that is, whether entities do or do not exist), the qualitative aspect too does not exhaust the matter: it may be the case that a pleasant life should not be lived if it ends in a way that is immoral. Call this the "teleological" dimension of the value of a life. We usually do not bring lives into the world with a plan, at least not for humans. Yet some plans constitute a misrecognition of what having a life means. Say someone brings me into the world for fifteen pleasant years, planning to euthanize me painlessly when these are over. Again, from an internal perspective, such a life is better than no life at all, and unlike being brought into the world to be a prostituted child, here such existence is qualitatively unproblematic. Still, no one would be justified in bringing people into the world with this purpose in mind.

The issue is not merely one of violating rights that are, let us assume, exclusive to humans. Such lives, human or nonhuman, should not be lived (to take our previous nonhuman example, say someone breeds dogs just to have the chance to painlessly euthanize young puppies). Teleological violations of life's value can then relate to the temporal length of that life. Accidental or natural premature death is sad for humans and nonhumans, though it is not immoral. But instituting a practice in which premature death is intended for the born entity is morally wrong and cannot be excused through the entity's gain by living. Teleological violations can also relate to manners of exploitation, and this too need not be associated with a qualitatively negative experience. The film *The Matrix* depicts a scenario in which human beings are brought into the world, lead monitored illusory lives from start to finish that can be pleasant, solely for the production of energy that their bodies create. Such living is better than not living at all, but it is not hard to imagine someone saying that such a life should not be lived.[9]

Vegetarian Utopia

Benefiting or harming a future life is, then, determined by three dimensions: the quantitative (that is, whether such a life exists), the qualitative (the nature of the future existence in terms of suffering vs. pleasure), and the teleological (whether a purpose projected onto the future life is morally objectionable as such even if it involves qualitatively satisfying existence). The three dimensions help us determine when the argument regarding benefiting animals by bringing them into existence is acceptable, and when it is a self-serving rationalization.

Vegans and vegetarians tell meat-eaters that eating flesh as means of helping animals to exist is a self-serving rationalization. Vegans level the same charge against ovo-lacto vegetarians who claim that their choice promotes a better world for animals. The tripartite division of life's value enables seeing why meat-eaters are indeed rationalizing, and why vegetarians are right. Any animal-related practice should be evaluated in terms of whether the lives it brings to the world should be lived. Having pets is continuous with quantitative and qualitative dimensions and does not constitute a morally objectionable life. It is accordingly an overall good practice for pets. Stuffing geese cannot be excused through saying that they get to live, since such lives are qualitatively horrifying. Breeding cows in order to kill them when they are a year or two old is a morally

---

[9] *Why* are such lives morally objectionable? Is there some inherent sanctity to life that is being violated? Can such sanctity be unpacked in secular terms? Is it the same for human and for nonhuman animals? I cannot enter such questions here. I will limit myself to the uncontroversial and shared objection to some uses of animals, even if they are qualitatively benign. People with different convictions and philosophies would object to euthanizing the puppies, and, for our purposes, we can avoid asking which is the best justification for this.

objectionable plan even when they do get to live pleasant lives (some calves do). On the other hand, sheering and milking sheep does not prevent them from leading a qualitatively good life, and so here the quantitative dimension does have weight: bringing such animals into the world can be an overall good for them. The same applies to harvesting eggs from hens and milk from cows, if these are kept in good conditions.

Reforming current exploitative farm-animal husbandry by turning such lives into qualitatively desirable lives is not limited to providing reasonable space for the animals. Avoiding killing animals when they are over their productive period probably implies that eggs and milk will be more expensive than they are today. (On the other hand, a pro-animal ideal state will also be one in which many more of these sources of protein will be consumed. Greater demand may compensate farmers for endorsing less economical breeding practices.) As for regulating the birth of "unproductive" male offspring in poultry and cows, here differential artificial insemination (which already exists technically) can create both an economical and a moral predifferentiation of livestock without killing. I see nothing against the practice of enhancing the animal's diet to make it more profitable for the farmer, as this need not occasion suffering. As for artificially induced consecutive pregnancies in cows, there is no reason to think that this practice harms the cow (women who have many children do not appear to live shorter lives or to suffer from long-term deficiencies).[10] Like pets, such animals can be euthanized when they are old or sick, and then (here I deviate from some moral vegetarians) no moral objection stands in the way of eating them or using their hides, or processing their carcasses into pet food. The difference between eating

---

[10] I have been unable to find an official assessment here. Dairy cows are the ones that get inseminated, and these are slaughtered when they are young (usually ages 4–6) when their milk production decreases. Such cows are impregnated throughout their lives, but since they do not live a full life, data supporting the damages of consecutive pregnancies are hard to find. Another factual lacuna in my argument that I would like to record is the incapacity to assess the necessity of separating cows from calves for the purpose of commercial milk-production and whether or not this separation causes suffering (rather than some momentary distress). It is not obvious to me that separation is mandatory. According to Dr. Nahum Shpigel, a farm-animal specialist at the Koret School of Veterinary Medicine, the amount of milk consumed by the younger calves is negligible, and the reason for the early separation of calves does not relate to reduced quantities of milk, but to preventing disease and injury should calves remain with mature animals. As calves grow to be several months old, their milk intake does become substantial, and, should farms strive to avoid separation, they would have to also devise methods for early weaning. Shpigel claims that any attempt to change the farms in order to avoid separation of calves (pigs, for example, are not separated from sows) would have to be radical in order to avoid injuries to calves, and this would inevitably lead to less expedient production. For vegetarian utopia this strikes me as good news, for while it means that factory-farming will have to be abolished, large-scale production of milk would still be feasible (like it was prior to factory-farms).

Second, there are considerations of effectiveness relative to the overall goals of pro-animal protest. Overdemanding strategic moves will decrease the number of protestors and thus diminish the overall effect of the protest. Veganism is a much more difficult lifestyle than ovo-lacto vegetarianism and raises many more nutritional concerns, especially when one is making dietary decisions not only for oneself.[11] Prudentially, animal welfare will lose many potential advocates if nothing less than highly demanding personal measures are demanded and made. Ergo: evaluated as a form of protest against existing conditions, tentative veganism is counterproductive to liberationism and, through that, detrimental to animal welfare.

The problem with this last antivegan argument is that the same criticism can be made against vegetarians by "demivegetarians" (people who eat meat only rarely). Demivegetarians will claim that vegetarianism demands too much and is counterproductive relative to their own milder form of protest. Against demivegetarians it should be pointed out that the difference between eating flesh and eating eggs is that both vegetarians and tentative vegans agree that the latter is essentially moral, whereas the former is not. "Essential" here means that for vegetarians, unlike eating eggs, under no conditions is it moral to kill an animal for the purpose of eating it when nutritional alternatives are available. Demivegetarianism is thus perhaps strategically prudential, but, like occasional molesting, it constitutes participation in a morally wrong act and is hence unjustified, whereas vegetarians that selectively eat eggs and dairy participate in a move forward.

Against this, tentative vegans will say that eating eggs may not be "essentially" wrong, but exploitation is an essential wrong, and that participating as a consumer with acts of lesser exploitation is still essentially wrong. To return to the analogy with slavery, abolitionism too no doubt appeared overdemanding, but the personal price a reform may exert cannot be a plausible objection to its moral standing. Doing the right thing is sometimes tough. Tentative vegans and vegetarians thus diverge radically in the way they describe consumption of free-roaming animal-derived products, and both seem to be correct: buying and eating such products can be described either as supporting reform or as supporting fig-leaf exploitation, and nothing in the actions themselves favors one of these descriptions.

---

[11] While dieticians no longer declare that a vegetarian diet is nutritionally deficient, my own experience with a vegetarian lifestyle for several years, both personally and as a parent of three children, has not been smooth. There seem to be significant differences among individuals and the efficiency with which they process food: my wife, who has been a vegetarian longer than any of us, suffers from no deficiencies, while two of my children as well as myself have had to occasionally take iron supplements, although we are all on the same diet.

This descriptive, or hermeneutic, dimension of the debate strikes me as unfruitful because nothing in the act turns one of these competing descriptions into a misdescription. On the other hand, the *political* considerations that underlie which of these descriptions one should prefer lead to a less aporetic stance. Political reform movements have faced the moral problem of cooperating with partial, nonsatisfactory reform steps many times. Feminism shows, for example, how step-by-step cooperation with partial improvements paved the way to radical reform. Urging women not to vote in the first election in which they were allowed to do so on the basis of protesting against the patriarchal system as such (or because women were not yet themselves eligible candidates) would have damaged the feminist cause. Recognition of the imperfection of an improvement does not necessarily entail banning cooperation. Rather, it manifests an appreciation of slow change and the need to persist in supporting moves forward. To conclude, against the tentative vegan's claim that vegetarians participate in an exploitative practice when they eat products that are derived from free-roaming animals, vegetarians say first that nothing in the consumption makes the vegan description of it more reasonable than the vegetarian one. Second, political considerations make the vegetarian description of selective-consumption-as-promoting-progress preferable to the overly purist stance of the vegan.

I asked how to formulate the distinction between legitimate as opposed to illegitimate cooperation with progressive yet still exploitative practices. The first condition was the magnitude of the step taken by the progressive institution, that is, whether it manifests a substantial or a trivial moral recognition. The second was the strategic benefits of cooperation versus noncooperation assessed in relation to the overall political objective. A third condition concerns the extremity of the loss experienced by the exploited entity as part of obtaining a particular product from it. If eggs had to be ripped out of the hen's body through a painful procedure, then to consume eggs would amount to being implicated in immoral cooperation. By eating such eggs, one would in effect be commissioning someone else to do the painful harvesting. Such is the case with eating flesh; not with milk or eggs. The animals do not appear to be harmed. Cooperating as a consumer with the particular "service" provided by the animal is thus categorically different from cooperating with services that do involve loss or pain.

True, farm-animal husbandry involves painful procedures (debeaking in poultry and horn removal in cows). Hens are debeaked to reduce cannibalism. Sometimes it is said that the crowded conditions cause cannibalism,[12]

---

[12] J. Bowler, ed., *The Vegetarian Handbook: The Guide to Living a Vegetarian Lifestyle* (The Vegetarian Society UK, 1990), 20.

but a breeder of free-roaming hens with whom I talked told me that cannibalism does not appear to depend on space, as his free-roaming hens can still peck each other to death. He believes that debeaking positively benefits the hens. Reforming farm-animal husbandry in the vegetarian utopia will look carefully into these practices, seeking alternative methods of achieving their goals with less suffering. As far as present conditions are concerned, we can say this: to the extent that debeaking or horn removal prevents injury to other farm animals, such actions become as legitimate as spaying and neutering pets: a price such animals pay for coexistence with humans. We are, again, "calling the shots," and this will repel those who read into these animals notions like autonomy. But calling the shots here seems beneficial to these animals.

OBLIGATIONS IN PRACTICE

Vegetarians are required to look for less exploitative products. How tough is this requirement? Are vegetarians obligated to go to any length or cost to obtain products derived from free-roaming animals? (In terms of cost, such products can cost up to two or three times more than ordinary products; in terms of accessibility, milk from free-roaming cows is very hard to find.) Need they always prefer restaurants that use such products no matter how inferior these may be to others? Can they purchase and eat eggs and dairy products that do not come from free-roaming animals?

"Cooperation" with practices in this matter boils down to buying and eating. These do not necessarily go together since one can purchase products for someone else to eat, and consume products that someone else has bought. Begin with the buying part. If one insists on buying the cheapest egg and dairy products, one is commissioning someone else to produce in the most economically efficient ways, and this can mean commissioning exploitation. Vegetarians are obligated to support products that present moral progress even if these cost more.[13]

How about purchasing and eating products that are not derived from free-roaming animals? I have, up to now, claimed that much of the force

[13] How much more? This question is not merely economical but also social. If free-roaming breeding yields products that are out of the reach of many, such will violate a different moral principle, namely, that a moral lifestyle cannot depend on a high income. It is also true, however, that many of the issues broached in this book only pertain to people who live in developed countries in which alternatives to exploiting animals can be devised. The recognition that some dilemmas within animal ethics mostly pertain to the affluent world does not, obviously, dissolve these dilemmas. Affluence opens up moral possibilities that have hitherto been foreclosed.

of vegetarianism in opposition to veganism involves the capacity to influence production through selective consumption. Does this mean that vegetarians can never purchase the products of factory-farms? I think that it does not, and that vegetarians can fall short of ideal selective consumption. The reason for this relates to the third condition above: taking eggs or milk does not create suffering and loss. Participating here is accordingly categorically different from participating in acts that do involve a harm being done. Vegetarians are obligated to a policy of conscious and selective purchasing, and to give moral production practices a chance even if these are more expensive. But the obligation to seek ways to minimize and eliminate exploitation does not extend to a complete ban.

Buying products that are not derived from free-range animals if alternatives are implausibly difficult to obtain is excusable.[14] Such participation is no more than "excusable" since consuming products that rely on exploitative practice (and that ultimately form a part of the flesh industry too by slaughtering the animals that produce the eggs and the milk) can never be unproblematic. Nor is it morally plain-sailing to purchase products derived from free-roaming animals (vegans do have a substantial moral point). But all this means no more than that the obligation to avoid the products of factory-farms is substantial. "Excusable" is a term that will be suspicious only to those who assume that protest is of an all-or-nothing nature (if one opposes some actions done by the army of one's country, one ought to refuse to be drafted; if one opposes some actions taken by one's government, one ought to morally evade paying taxes, etc.). Why should we suppose that protest has this all-or-nothing character?

Boycotting products that do not involve suffering strikes me as a disproportionate form of protest. Deciding whether an act of protest is or is not "disproportionate" is not arbitrary. Everyone will agree that some

[14] Philosophers will want to know more about "excuses" and when they are morally acceptable. Call "saints" those who not only always fulfill their obligations, but also go beyond the call of duty and perform many substantial supererogatory actions. Call "angels" those who always act according to their moral obligations. Excuses come in at the next level, the one in which normal mortals operate, those who sometimes fail to act according to what they perceive as their duty. Some such obligations can never be avoided, and failing them cannot be excused (the obligation to avoid cruelty, for example). Excuses apply to lesser obligations and may be credibly employed when (a) the parties involved agree that the obligation that was not met belongs to this milder category; (b) the person making the excuse knows where his duty lies and that he is falling short of his moral obligation; (c) the person does regularly fulfill this duty rather than systematically disregards it; (d) the person has tried to avoid this failure (when possible); (e) the person has expressed regret or a willingness to compensate the injured party (when possible). Needless to say, (a)–(e) do not determine that a given excuse needs to be accepted. These characterizations merely suggest when reasons for action can qualify as excuses.

types of pro-animal protest are moral overkills (not talking to meat-eaters; not letting one's children play with the children of a farm owner; leaving one's town because a new abattoir has opened). Determining what makes for "reasonable" protest is not mysterious and involves straightforward considerations. Morally informed consumer actions have to retain some plausible relation with the suffering involved. The considerations that determine the plausibility of a form of protest include effectiveness, the ideal being envisaged, the need to balance one's morals with other goals, whether the specific sphere of action involved is one in which nothing less than doing the best will do, whether the act turns one's protest into an antisocial eccentric act, thus diminishing the political force of one's ideological agenda. and so on.

In focusing on suffering and loss as the important moral factors, in focusing on promoting morally better farm-animal husbandry through selective purchasing, vegetarians maintain a plausible relationship between their protest and their consumption. To conclude: there are limits to what is required of vegetarians. The best a moral vegetarian can do is to eat only products that come from free-roaming breeding. Purchasing and consuming other products is still excusable.[15]

---

[15] A reviewer of this book has suggested that this last discussion can fruitfully be covered by the distinction between what we do and what we allow. Yet "allowing" connotes (for me) an acceptance that the uneasiness of "excuses" avoids. In this area it is important to underscore and preserve the uneasiness and to rely on moral terms that register it.

Chapter 7

THERAPEUTIC USE

NONHUMAN ANIMAL-ASSISTED THERAPY (AAT) is becoming increasingly popular.[1] Expositors claim that its roots go back to the eighteenth century when Tuke, one of the originators of modern psychiatry, introduced dogs in his work with his patients. Nowadays, AAT encompasses interventions incorporating dogs, cats, rodents, birds, reptiles, horses, monkeys, and even dolphins. The goals of such therapy are extremely varied, including psychological therapeutic objectives, as well as other forms of assistance.[2]

---

[1] The literature deploys a finer terminology here, distinguishing AAT from AAA (animal-assisted activities), the latter covering nontherapeutic work conducted with animals that is nevertheless deemed potentially beneficial for humans. This distinction is not pertinent to the following analysis, so I will use AAT as an umbrella term covering various modalities of therapy and assistance incorporating the use of animals.

[2] Psychologically oriented AAT includes child-oriented interventions that rely on animals to achieve wide-ranging goals. These include boosting the self-esteem of insecure children through therapeutic horseback riding (hippotherapy); creating oblique communication over the child's own problems through interaction with animals; cultivating self-control and curtailing impulsive behavior in children with ADHD; and enhancing empathy, responsibility, and the child's capacity to nurse by creating controlled child-animal relationships. Psychological variants of AAT also include interventions with clinically depressed individuals, older people, and inmates in some prisons. In all, advocates of AAT claim that the capacity of animals to generate unconditional acceptance and to facilitate nonthreatening dialogue, their capacity to enforce a compelling "here and now" on individuals who are depressed or recuperating, even the tactile sensations that their touch induces, turn animals into invaluable helpers in creating therapeutically meaningful interventions. Some psychotherapists believe that, apart from allowing people to relate to themselves through projection, animals tap into various unconscious drives that they embody or archetypically signify, thus creating analytically deep therapy that could not be achieved through non-animal-targeted projections. Forms of AAT have also been introduced to assist people with disabilities (i.e., "service animals," such as dogs for individuals who are hearing impaired, guide dogs for blind people, monkeys for quadriplegic individuals). Animals feature in programs designed to assist people with mental disabilities. They are deployed as part of new modalities of speech therapy. Dogs are also relied upon to function as organic alarm systems that can help with specific medical conditions such as epilepsy and diabetes by alerting the owner to an oncoming seizure. Specialized animal-assisted therapy programs exist for retarded individuals, for autistic people, and for patients suffering from fatal incurable diseases. There are many available expositions of the current extent of AAT, as well as summaries of research that attempts to validate it. For some of these, see O. Cusack, *Pets and Mental Health* (New York: Haworth Press, 1988); R. Gilshtrom, *Special Pets for Special Needs Population* (Haifa: Ach, 2003) (in Hebrew); J. Grammonley et al., *Animal-Assisted Therapy: Therapeutic Interventions* (Bellevue, WA: Delta Society, 1997); A. Shalev, *The Furry Healer: Pets as a Therapeutic Means: Theory, Research and Practice* (Tel-Aviv: Tcherikover Publishers, 1996) (in Hebrew).

In this chapter, I will ignore the prudential questions that haunt most AAT literature I have come across, that is, whether the benefits of AAT can be conclusively shown over and against more conventional modes of therapy. I will assume—what is in fact highly controversial—that AAT is therapeutically effective generally and, for some individuals, is advantageous when compared with other forms of therapy. Can such uses of nonhuman animals be morally justified from a "liberationist" perspective, a perspective, that is, that acknowledges that animals are not merely a resource to be exploited by humans?

The Case against AAT

AAT literature does not ignore the moral dimension of the work that it advocates. Yet the remarks on ethics appear to be limited to considerations of welfare. The Delta Society's website, for example, cautions its readers that:

AAT may be inappropriate for the animals when

- Injuries from rough handling or from other animals may occur.
- Basic animal welfare cannot be assured. This includes veterinary care, and access to water and exercise areas.
- The animal does not enjoy visiting.

In a different publication by the same organization, it is maintained that "At all times the rights of the animals shall be respected and ensured. This includes humane treatment, protection from undue stress, and availability of water and exercise area."[3] One proposed code of ethics for animal-assisted therapy includes the requirements that the animal's welfare must be the priority of the therapy facilitator; the therapy animal must "never be forced to leave the home to go to work" or to perform actions it is reluctant to perform; and animals are to be given adjustment time and quiet-time periods before sessions and be protected from individuals carrying diseases that may be transmitted to them.[4] Yet, from a broader liberationist perspective, such remarks barely scratch the surface of the moral questions that AAT raises. A liberationist stance ascribes value not only to the life of the animal, but also to the quality of such a life, as well as to the value of the animal's freedom, in the sense that restricting freedom requires a moral justification. For

---

[3] Gammonley et al., *Animal-Assisted Therapy*, 2.

[4] R. J. Preziosi, "For your Consideration: A Pet Assisted Therapist Facilitator Code of Ethics," *The Latham Letter* (Spring 1997): 5–6.

liberationists, using animals to treat humans is potentially immoral in six distinct ways:

1. *Limitations of freedom*: Animals need to be kept by the therapists or be temporary companion animals of the individual being treated, or the disabled individual being helped. In some cases, when the animals are in effect modified pets (like guide dogs), the limitations of freedom are the same as those involved in all owner-pet relationships (relationships that are themselves immoral for some liberationists regardless of their quality, though not for the liberationist stance taken by this book). In the case of animals that are not pets or modified pets (e.g., rabbits, hamsters, chinchillas, snakes, and birds), the loss of freedom may be much more severe. All of these respond to human beings but, unlike alarm or service dogs, they do not appear to derive pleasure from such interaction and seem incapable of transferring their social needs—for those of them that do exhibit such—onto humans.

2. *Life determination*: Freedom can be curtailed for a temporary period (for example, confining a wounded animal that lives in the wild, and then releasing it once it has healed). But unlike type 1 actions, some actions with regard to animals are total and life determining. Turning an animal into a companion animal, into a zoo animal, a race horse, a jumper, or an event horse are life-determining actions. The decision to employ an animal therapeutically involves making such a total decision regarding a particular animal.

3. *Training*: Getting dogs or monkeys to efficiently assist humans in numerous tasks involves a prolonged training period, which itself includes various violations of the animal's well-being. Creating therapy-horses requires "breaking" them. Moreover, unlike cats and dogs, many of the other animals used in AAT are frightened by human presence and have to undergo periods in which they get accustomed to humans around them.

4. *Social disconnection*: Simians live in packs. By turning them into nursing entities, one disconnects them from whatever it is that they maintain through their social context. The same holds for rabbits or other rodents that are isolated from their kin. There is, to be sure, a certain degree of mystery here regarding both the nature of the social needs and the way they might be internally experienced as a loss by the animal. Yet it is dubious to deny that such disconnection (or bringing up the animal without contact with its kin) is a form of deprivation.

5. *Injury*: Therapy animals can be (and are) routinely manhandled. Even when they are gently handled, exposing them to strangers who pet them can itself induce anxieties in them. A small percentage of such animals are injured during these sessions.[5]

---

[5] Most surveys on AAT given above describe cases of manhandling and injury.

6. *Instrumentalization*: Liberationists tend to tacitly or explicitly model ideal human-animal relations on analogies with human-human ethics. While few extend to animals the same range of moral considerability that befits humans, liberationists turn the human-animal model from the thoughtless instrumentalization that is typical of human relations with objects into forms of interaction that approximate human-human relations. From this perspective, since it is unimaginable to retain a subgroup of human beings as therapeutic aids of other human beings even if proved as facilitating extremely effective therapy (say that the tactile quality of touching members of this subgroup is proved to have therapeutic merits), doing this to animals is wrong in a similar way. Animals are not out there to be used by us, even when the use is important or worthy.

Liberationists would be quick to identify these six potential violations of the moral status of animals and would accordingly be concerned about the moral legitimacy of AAT as such. The fact that much more serious violations than the uses described in 1–6 occur in relation to animals does not abrogate the moral questions that relate to types 1–6. It matters not that billions of animals are routinely killed for negligible reasons, or that they are institutionally used and exploited in large-scale industries all over the world. If types 1–6 cannot be vindicated, liberationists should censor these modalities of therapy and assistance.

A Paternalistic Case for AAT?

Analyzing the moral status of types 1–6 invites an exploration of the owner-pet relationship. If such relationships can be morally justified, some of the therapeutic uses of animals sketched above might be vindicated as well.[6] In the previous chapter I proposed a utilitarian-based justification of the owner-pet relationship that can morally legitimate the practice of keeping some animals as pets. In a nutshell, my claim was that the hands-off approach advocated by some liberationists—the idea that the lives of animals are better the less paternalistic they are—is morally sound though, ironically, not always in the interest of the animals themselves. Accordingly, liberationists should avoid the hands-off

---

[6] A different possible moral extension of considerations, which I will not attempt, relates to zoos. If keeping animals in zoos is not immoral, curtailing their movement when they are placed in pet centers and making life-determining decisions for them when turning them into therapeutic means will surely pass as moral too. I will avoid this direction because reversing these transitive relations does not work: a justification of animal therapy is not, a fortiori, a vindication of zoos, and I wish to retain the possibility that animal therapy is a justified practice whereas the other is not. The moral status of zoos is discussed in the next chapter.

approach. With regard to companion animals, some owner-pet relation-ships are an overall good for human as well as for nonhuman animals. The paternalistic framework of such relations is a potential wrong but is exonerated because it makes for a better world for small animals: it is an overall better alternative for them than a life in the wild. Success stories of feral populations of horses and dogs would modify such an impres-sion only in a few examples but are less impressive when thinking about highly populated countries, in which such animals would turn into "pests" and would be treated accordingly. Cats and dogs get to lead longer, safer, and more comfortable lives, and, while they lose through this exchange too (loss of freedom, being subjected to various operative interventions), such losses are offset by the benefits to them in the long run (limiting movement can prolong the life of the pet since it diminishes the risks of accidents and injury from fighting other animals, a neutered animal lives longer). In other cases, such losses help preserve the owner-pet relations as such (most owners would refuse to keep animals that can freely reproduce), relations that are themselves an overall good for the pet. I claimed that such welfare-based thinking can also generate welfare-based distinctions that can tell us when pet abuse takes place and can guide some moral decision making within small animal veterinary medi-cine. Some paternalistic, invasive owner actions are justified on welfare grounds because the overall good for companion animals trumps their resistance to the action (e.g., vaccination). Other such actions are obvi-ously immoral, since they do not promote any animal interest and ad-vance a marginal interest of the owner (e.g., ear docking). Most other ac-tions fall in the middle and should be assessed in terms of the overall good for the animal and for the owner, and in terms of available alterna-tives to the examined action. For some animals, turning them into com-panion animals is not a benefit to them in any obvious way (wild animals and birds), and so welfare considerations urge us to oppose attempts to keep such animals as pets. Yet the same considerations suggest that the practice of keeping companion animals is not objectionable as such: an ideal liberationist world will include owner-pet relationships, and such relations, at their best, also show us that a paternalistic yet nonexploita-tive human-animal relation is both possible and actual.

Can animal therapy be justified in a similar way? "Service" animals such as signal and guide dogs easily fall into the owner-pet category, and so such practices are in principle justified. Dogs do pay a price for such lives: they are spayed or neutered, trained for long periods (in the case of guide dogs, much longer than other dogs), and isolated from their kin. But dogs seem to be able to transfer their social needs onto humans, and some of the prolonged training can arguably be an advantage, pro-viding important (and pleasurable) mental stimulation to these dogs. If humanity were to endorse a hands-off approach with regard to animals, such dogs would appear to lead qualitatively inferior (and probably shorter) lives in the wild, even in the few countries in the world in which the notion of "the wild" still makes sense. Some AAT programs strive to connect animal interests and human needs by placing shelter animals with older people, thus benefiting particular animals in an even more immediate way.[7] Is a capuchin monkey, captured in the wild, isolated from its pack, trained using electric shocks, teeth extracted—all of these prior to placing it as a nurse of a disabled person—better off than living in the wild?[8] The answer is negative. Such an animal is better off if it has nothing to do with humans. In such examples the hands-off approach is not only morally sound but also continuous with the animal's welfare. The same holds for other forms of AAT: maintaining stressed rodents in petting areas in educational and therapeutic institutions for the projected benefit of children, psychiatric patients, or prisoners who may enjoy various therapeutic benefits through this connection does not appear to promote any of the rodent's own interests.[9] The lives of these rodents apart from humans appear to be a better alternative for them.

The same considerations help make sense of horse-assisted therapy. Justifying hippotherapy brings up the range of moral issues relating to equine husbandry and the moral status of the diverse practices that it involves (racing, show jumping, dressage, hunting, riding as such). Training horses requires lengthy instruction periods and the use of bits, whips, and harnesses. Many of them are then kept in very small locks. They are subjected to all of the medical interventions that cats and dogs undergo. All of these practices would disturb liberationists. Yet where and how would horses exist in an ideal liberationist world? Reserves might be an option in some countries in which feral populations of horses might be feasible. But in many parts of the world, a puritanical decision to let horses be would boil down to a horseless environment.

Liberationists would know that the argument from the animal's projected welfare is a risky one to make, since the idea that the animal's existence justifies exploiting it is routinely invoked in various forms, supposedly vindicating all kinds of animal abuse. However, I believe that in the context of AAT this justification is viable. I do wish to add, though, that since equine husbandry appears to be economically driven through

---

[7] A program discussed in D. Lannuzi and A. N. Rowan, "Ethical Issues in Animal-Assisted Therapy Programs," *Anthrozoös* 4 (3) (1991): 154–63.

[8] For details of this program, see ibid.

[9] The surveys on AAT cited above usually comment on the stress and anxiety that may be involved in such programs (see, in particular, ibid.). Animals have desires and needs, though some philosophers doubt whether these constitute interests. This subtlety does not affect my arguments throughout this book.

and through, the idea that some relations between humans and horses are justified in the sense that they ultimately benefit horses does not morally cleanse all such relationships. It is not obvious to me that practices such as racing, dressage, or show jumping are morally justified, since they involve pain and risk of injury to the animal and, according to Dr. Orit Zamir (DVM), can radically curtail the life span of the horse and diminish its quality. Hippotherapy, by contrast, is not a form of human-animal connection that appears detrimental to the horse. The utilitarian benefits for such horses—they get to exist, lead safe and relatively comfortable lives, are not abused or exploited—outweigh the price they pay.

USE VERSUS EXPLOITATION

I have so far argued that for some animals, AAT cannot be vindicated by appeals to the overall good for the animal through its forced participation in a paternalistic relationship with humans. Could some other framework justify using animals for therapeutic purposes? In this section I will discuss (and reject) two such possible justifications: Cartesianism and Kantianism. Later I address utilitarianism and speciesism.

Cartesians claim that animals lack moral considerability. For a Cartesian, it is senseless to draw a morally relevant distinction between animals and objects (for Descartes this also involved a denial of animal pain). Since moral considerations do not apply to animals, any action done to them—AAT included—is morally permissible. Kantians are fig-leaf Cartesians. They agree with Cartesians that animals are not the kind of beings that can be morally maltreated by virtue of what they are. But they also claim that some actions with respect to animals are morally reprehensible. This stems not from anything having to do with the animal itself, but from how such actions define the agents that performed them: from what these actions say about them or about humanity in general. Cartesians would have no problem with any form of AAT since, for them, animals are no more than means to an end. Kantians would concur with this, adding the restriction that no abuse or cruelty should take place as part of AAT. (Consistent Cartesians would have no problem with "cruelty" to therapy animals—they would object to the use of term as well, "cruelty" exemplifying a category mistake in this context—if it is shown to be therapeutically beneficial to human patients).[10]

---

[10] While Cartesians seem to be more hostile than Kantians to the liberationist cause, it is interesting to note that Descartes' own position, resting as it did on the denial of animal pain, is thus conditional on an empirical belief that, when informed (and transformed) by our modern understanding regarding pain, would change the moral attitude toward animals. By contrast, the Kantian indirect duties approach thoroughly banishes animals from

The more general issue of the moral considerability of animals was presented in the first part of this book and need not be rehashed now. In our context, both Cartesians and Kantians constitute a theoretical, not a practical, opposition. By this I mean that judging by the literature they produce and by their concern with animal welfare, people involved in offering AAT appear to be both sensitive and concerned about the well-being of the animals they rely on. They would find it odd to think that one may do anything one likes to an animal (Cartesianism), or that torturing a dog is wrong not because of the dog, but only because of what this says about the torturer (Kantianism).

Short of categorically ostracizing animals from the pale of moral concern, AAT advocates may try to defend the idea that using animals is permissible, even when detrimental to their welfare, so long as no abuse takes place. They will argue that such use does not constitute exploitation. This move can succeed only partially in light of the use/exploitation distinction offered in chapter 5. The gist of the distinction was that you use an entity if your actions in relation to it are calculated to promote your own interests. You exploit an entity if such self-serving actions are severely detrimental to the well-being of the entity. Use is legitimate; exploitation is not. Applied to AAT, this means that service dogs are used, though not exploited, since their welfare is promoted by the relationship. Horses too gain much from their relations with humans. The same cannot be said for rodents, snakes, birds, aquarium-kept dolphins, or monkeys, who gain little or nothing through AAT and lose a lot.[11] Unlike horses or dogs, all of these creatures can easily exist in the wild in large numbers, and by turning them into vehicles for therapy, both their freedom and their social needs are radically curtailed. Counter to my hypothetical critic's claims, AAT that uses these creatures is exploitative and is to be eradicated, even if no abuse takes place.

Two Objections

Before examining whether exploiting animals can be defended as such, I need to respond to two counterarguments to what I have just said. The

---

the pale of moral concern, and this dismissal is unconnected to the existence or nonexistence of animal pain. The awareness that animals produce and respond to endorphins, that they respond to pain relievers, etc., probably would have persuaded Descartes to modify his position. Kant, on the other hand, would have been unimpressed.

[11] It was pointed out to me that in some dolphin-related AAT programs the dolphins are actually free, and the therapeutic objectives are obtained without moving the dolphins from their natural habitat and without coercion. My remarks throughout this chapter regarding dolphins do not apply to such programs.

first is that I am downplaying the significance of the price horses and dogs pay for their existence in the company of humans. Watching a horse struggle with the bit in its mouth is a difficult sight. "Breaking" horses or the prolonged training periods that service dogs undergo can boil down to painful activities and deprivation, especially when the training system is not (or is not only) reward based. Moreover, the import of thwarting the procreative potential of these animals by sterilizing them cannot be ignored. The second objection has to do with the argument from nonexistence that I relied on when claiming that dogs and horses gain from their relations with humans since this relationship means that they exist. I have referred to my previous defense of the metaphysical plausibility of such an argument. (In a nutshell, I argued that a nonexistent entity cannot be harmed by not bringing "it" into existence, yet it—now without the quotes—can benefit from a decision to bring it into existence. There is nothing contradictory about an entity having both these properties.) But there is a non-metaphysically based objection to this move having to do with species as opposed to particular entities. I said that in most countries, horses and dogs are not likely to exist outside of use-based human relations and that abrogating all such relations will in any case imply a radical reduction in the number of such beings. But an AAT therapist can choose to breed particular rodents for the purpose of using them in therapeutic sessions, claiming that like horses or dogs, these *particular* animals gain their existence from entering this exchange. Why, then, am I legitimating the former relations and opposing the latter?

Beginning with the substantial price that horses and dogs pay for living their lives with humans, here a liberationist is compelled to factor in moral, political, and strategic considerations. The previous chapter's comparison between vegan and vegetarian utopia holds here too: the vegetarian ideal, which allows for some use-based relations with animals, is overall better for animals than the vegan ideal. Many more animals would exist (millions more would exist), the lives they would lead would be qualitatively good ones, and this would not exemplify a perverse perception of animal lives being merely means for producing this or that. And it is such a world that liberationists should strive to create. This does not obviously legitimize everything done to dogs or horses. Some aesthetic surgery for dogs cannot be legitimated, and some modes of keeping and using horses will disappear. But this position involves embracing a quasi-paternalistic relationship with these beings, holding that doing so is beneficial to them. For a liberationist, the moral price of accepting this position is upholding the moral legitimacy of bits, harnesses, whips, and invasive surgery. Yet for liberationists such as myself, the moral price that the first world implies, although more abstract in nature, is higher: one has to, in this case, swallow the implications of a petless world, both in terms of ourselves and of these beings. And since the lives of many horses and pets are qualitatively good ones, I do not subscribe to the morally purer stance that will make all of these disappear.

Responding to the second counterargument requires specifying when and where the argument from nonexistence can be legitimately employed. Merely bringing a being into existence is not, ipso facto, a benefit to it. Two additional considerations have to be brought into play before one can conclude that an entity benefits from bringing it into existence. First, the qualitative consideration: if the entity's future life is predicted to be qualitatively bad in a significant way, then bringing it into existence is not a benefit to it. The negative quality has to, of course, be significant. An obvious example is that of bringing a person into a long life of perpetual torture.[12] The second consideration is "teleological": bringing a being into a life form that is objectionable, even if the life offered is qualitatively reasonable—for example, bringing some people with a rare blood type into the world with the sole purpose of using them as donors later (while providing them with a qualitatively reasonable existence). I call this consideration "teleological" because here the problem is with the morally distorted projected goal for a life.

I have claimed that in the case of rodents, birds, reptiles, fish, and monkeys, there is no species-related, welfare-based justification that enables perceiving AAT as a practice that helps these beings qua members of a potentially extinct species. The counterargument has granted this yet claimed that bringing a *particular* member of these animals into existence for the purpose of AAT benefits it. In response, I admit that the AAT therapist who brings a particular rodent to life for the purpose of AAT does not necessarily abuse it. The life of the rodent may be comfortable, and it need not constitute a perverse life-goal in the same manner in which, say, factory-farming abuses the lives of the animals that it utilizes. However, that a particular rodent does benefit from the decision to bring it into existence should not modify the conclusion for a liberationist. The reason

---

[12] This claim has no implication for discussions of euthanasia (assuming that animal-ethics discussions carry over into human ethics). The considerations that pertain to a future life that no one yet has are different from those that are relevant to a life that is already possessed by a particular person. One cannot be said to benefit a future potential life by bringing it into a projected life of perpetual fear, isolation, and pain. This does not imply that someone who already lives such a life is better off dead. The claim is also disconnected from the abortion debate, which includes its own claims regarding the relative quality of a future life. An existing zygote is a particular potential/actual life, while we are here considering abstract potential ones. Moreover, the two considerations that prompt future quality-of-life arguments within the abortion debate (the negative quality of a future life of disability, and the negative effects of being adopted when one's biological parents cannot responsibly function as parents) are categorically distinct from issues of projected future exploitation that are relevant here.

for this is that when a particular AAT animal's welfare is genuinely considered, it seems overall best for it to be set free *after* it has been brought into existence by the therapist. And so, if the technician is truly concerned with the particular animal's welfare, she should hypothetically release it from captivity as soon as possible. Unlike dogs or horses, the release of which either is not feasible in most areas (horses) or appears to compromise their welfare, mice, hamsters, and chinchillas on the whole express no particular attachment to human contact (unlike dogs) nor seek their company (unlike some cats). And so, a particular, welfare-based justification from nonexistence can succeed only if one is willing to accept the implication that the same welfare considerations that justify bringing the particular animal into existence also undermine maintaining an AAT-based relationship with this particular animal, since releasing it is overall better for it.

Further Objections (and Conclusion)

Animals cannot be excluded from moral consideration. This means, among other things, that there is a moral obligation to circumvent either-or conflicts of interest between humans and animals. This obligation undermines speciesist or utilitarian objections to my general claim regarding AAT. In our context a speciesist rejoinder—upholding the wrong kind of speciesism—would boil down to saying that since human interests are more important than the interests of animals, various forms of exploitation (such as the forms of AAT that utilize rodents, birds, dolphins, reptiles, and monkeys) are morally permissible. Apart from relying on a fallacy that I have repeatedly underscored in this book—the illegitimate move from superiority to harm—the move cannot be marshaled in the context of AAT. The question is not whose interests are more important, but whether a particular conflict of interest can be avoided. Since the either-or nature of the question of some forms of AAT is a mirage, speciesism is continuous with abrogating forms of AAT that involve exploitation and can be easily superseded by other forms of therapy, including forms of non-exploitative AAT.

Utilitarian objections to the foregoing conclusion are similar, basically contending that the overall good achieved in a world in which exploitative forms of AAT occur is greater than the overall good within a world that excludes such therapeutic options. Unpacking "overall good" shows that, in the AAT context, there are three possible variants of the utilitarian claim, two of which are speciesist, the third liberationist. The two speciesist variants of this utilitarian argument would hold that human interests are more important than animal interests. They would differ on what "more important" should mean in practice, the first variant holding that any human interest categorically trumps any animal one. The second variant maintains that some human interests trump some (though not all) animal ones.[13] The liberationist variant of a utilitarian objection—which is actually continuous with classical utilitarianism—is that human and nonhuman interests count equally, yet it may be the case that some disutility to animals occasioned by exploitative forms of AAT substantially promotes the well-being of some humans in a way that makes for a better world than one in which exploitation does not occur.

Responding to these objections need not invoke the complex evaluation of utilitarianism as such or the difficulties involved in weighing interests. If my previous argument is sound, considerations of an overall good only superficially imply that anyone's interests should be compromised, so all three utilitarian variants miss the mark. The therapeutic benefits to humans could be achieved without exploitation either through alternative forms of therapy or through forms of AAT that use horses, cats, or dogs. Accordingly, avoiding the use of the other therapy animals as part of AAT does not diminish the projected overall good.

In conclusion: forms of AAT that rely on horses and dogs are continuous with the welfare of these animals. Without a relationship with humans, an overwhelming number of these beings would not exist. Their lives with human beings exact a price from them. But given responsible human owners, such lives are qualitatively comfortable and safe and need not frustrate the social needs of these creatures. A world in which practices like AAT exist is an overall better world for these beings than one that does not include them, and this provides a broad moral vindication of forms of AAT that depend on these beings. On the other hand, rodents, birds, monkeys, reptiles, and dolphins gain little by coercing them into AAT. Such practices are therefore exploitative. Since the human interests that are involved can be easily met without exploiting these beings, the moral conclusion is that such forms of AAT should be abolished.

[13] For this distinction, see Brody, "Defending Animal Research."

Chapter 8

RECREATIONAL USE

THE DISTINCTION BETWEEN use and exploitation underlies this section of the book and is a cardinal one for any comprehensive moral outlook on our relations with nonhuman animals. It is possible to map onto the use/exploitation opposition the three diverging perspectives in debates over animals that are under human supervision: (1) animals are never exploited—merely used; (2) animals are never used—always exploited; (3) some animals are used by humans while others are exploited by them. The first position holds that by virtue of what they are, nonhuman animals can never be exploited (or, what boils down to the same: they can be exploited, but such exploitation is not morally problematic). The second group perceives any self-serving relationship with animals as exploitative, even when it significantly promotes the interests of animals in such relationships. This position prescribes moral veganism and opposes maintaining companion animals. The third group does not rule out all animal-related practices yet is willing to abrogate some of them, if they constitute exploitation.

This book advocates the perspective of the third group. I find its outlook attractive, since it accommodates the possibility that some human-animal relations can be morally blameless. Such relationships benefit both humans and nonhumans and can potentially be vindicated when generalized into large-scale practices. The other advantage of (3) is that it also facilitates the recognition that nonhuman animals may be exploited, and that animal-related practices can be morally wrong even if they do not involve palpable cruelty and suffering. For both these reasons, should it prevail, (3) will substantially improve the overall lot of animals. And (3) is also a less radical stance than the one adopted by the second group, making it strategically more feasible by enabling liberationism to appeal to a larger consensus. Some may also find it to be ecologically more responsible than its more radical alternatives.

The problem for endorsers of (3)—call them "moderate liberationists"—is how to avoid a programmatic stance that lacks substantial coordinates able to successfully differentiate exploitation from use. The challenge relates first to clarifying the conceptual distinction between use and exploitation as such; second, to showing how this distinction pertains to nonhuman animals; and third, to applying this distinction to actual animal-related practices, respecting their particular nature and the conduct they involve and, in particular, how these practices might be advancing the interests of some animals. The implications of such clarification are far reaching, relating to what we eat, wear, or regard as entertainment. Previously in this book, I evaluated the practice of using farm animals, as well as the practice of using animals as therapeutic means. In this chapter I consider the welfare-based defense of zoos: a defense that attempts to morally vindicate zoos by arguing that the interests of animals kept in land or aquatic zoos are promoted by good zoos. I follow the stages above: explicating the use/exploitation distinction, applying it to animals, and turning finally to examining the variant of the argument that harnesses this distinction to mobilize a moral defense of zoos.

Use/Exploitation and Justifying Paternalism

To facilitate examining the moral status of zoos, here is a summary of my earlier justification for using animals in general. Give-and-take relations among humans are morally acceptable under various restrictions. This means that mutual use need not constitute exploitation. Given informed consent, given the existence of actual choice among genuine available alternatives, given that the transaction does not itself impose some morally distorted objective onto the life of one of the parties, there is nothing immoral in such exchanges. In the case of humans, consent, choice, and respect are themselves derived from more overarching considerations pertaining to what may not be done to human beings. Restrictions on human-related action are not a moral outcropping issuing out of elements external to them (e.g., their value to other human beings). Such restrictions are implied by what humans themselves possess, by what they are. Theories would here differ on whether possessing interests, or rights, some intrinsic value, or the capacity to suffer, or to generate value judgments, are the deeper elements that we recognize and ascribe to humans that, in turn, give rise to these restrictions.

Sometimes we ignore the desires of human beings and disregard the inability to obtain their consent, yet feel that such practice is morally legitimate. Children, or variously incapacitated individuals, are sometimes treated in such ways. The justification for ignoring their autonomy appeals to the action performed as being beneficial to these people. Paternalism is thus morally exonerated by perceiving paternal relations as increasing overall welfare, and/or eliminating impending harms that the person cannot yet (or ever) fathom, because of either age or ailment. Paternalism to children involves the expectation that they eventually grow out of such relationships and become autonomous.

Our relations with nonhuman animals are many times modeled on a paternalistic framework. Companion animals are the most obvious example. Being vaccinated, spayed, or neutered, limited in movement, and trained are done without the consent of such animals, but by calling the shots for them, deciding what is in their (and our) best interest. Such relationships are paternalistic, and, unlike the case of children, they remain paternalistic. When questioned, the source of the moral legitimacy of such relationships is that companion animals gain substantially from such lives, that they do not lose much, and that such living is not some deep perversion of what they are (I am thinking of actions like caging a bird). Remaining within this consensus, it appears that paternalistic relations with regard to nonhuman animals can be vindicated if predicated on the animal's projected welfare.

If keeping companion animals is justified, our best defense for this practice (and it does require a defense once we abandon the belief that we are simply entitled to do so by virtue of what we and they are) underscores the promotion of the welfare of those animals: they get to live and to lead comfortable and safe lives. Such reasoning, when applied to an animal-related practice, constitutes "a welfare-based defense." The question for liberationists is how broad this permission for paternalism actually is. The question of scope relates both to species types and to specific actions done to particular animals. Can paternalism to pets be legitimately extended to farm and zoo animals? To all? To some? And which particular actions does such paternalism justify? (Spaying? Vaccinating? Isolating? Training? Debeaking?)

In my analysis of the moral viability of extending petlike paternalistic conceptualizations to farm animals, I claimed that given reform, the relations between humans and farm animals can be maintained to the mutual benefit of both. Humans will be using such animals. But such use need not constitute exploitation so long as the animal's welfare is being substantially boosted. If the lives of such animals are qualitatively satisfying (in a way that will have to be well defined), such relationships are morally vindicated. Aside from various qualifications of this general claim, I argued that the most important gain for farm animals is that billions of qualitatively good lives can be lived through this forced exchange, whereas the alternative is a world in which these creatures would hardly exist at all. Feral populations of cows, hens, and pigs can be imagined and perhaps actualized in some parts of the world. Yet if many more such creatures can live qualitatively good lives among humans to the benefit of both humans and animals, legitimating such human-nonhuman relations is an overall good for these beings. Given reform, paternalism with regard to farm animals can be justified. Can zoos be likewise vindicated?

The Welfare-Based Defense of Zoos

The most elaborate and substantial presentation of a welfare-based defense of zoos is Stephen Bostock's *Zoos and Animal Rights*.[1] Bostock's
case on behalf of zoos intriguingly attempts to forge a link between an
animal-right perspective and a welfare-based argument for the existence
of (good) zoos. In sum: good zoos prop up the overall welfare of most of
the animals they keep. While, in Bostock's view, animals have a right to
freedom, this need not mean that violating this right is immoral. For
Bostock, as long as the welfare needs of a particular zoo animal are ac-
commodated, we are justified in holding that life in captivity is in that
animal's interest (46). Bostock foregrounds the vagueness of the term
"wild." He questions the assumptions that zoos keep wild animals (since
in modern zoos most animals are already born in captivity). He then
broaches a detailed and informed examination whether wild animals are
better off in the wild.

Bostock points out that zoos provide animals with a longer life, one
that benefits from veterinary care. He qualifies this evaluation by pointing out various ailments and diseases that zoos may be inducing in their
underexercised inmates. Bostock maintains that on the whole, the rule
should be that a wild animal is better off left in the wild (75). His
conclusion is mild: sometimes this latter rule does not apply; for some
animals the benefits of captivity make for a beneficial trade-off. Since
everything turns on what "promotion" of welfare could plausibly mean,
Bostock focuses on various competing criteria that could substantiate assumptions regarding what counts as advancing (or demoting) an animal's welfare. For him, the most defensible criteria are an amalgam of
several considerations, the main ones being health (longevity, physical
and mental well-being), breeding, and preserving natural behavior (along
with a corresponding lack of abnormal behavior).

Bostock believes in animal rights. It is therefore fair to challenge his
position through counterexamples invoking the analogy to other right-
possessing entities, namely, human beings. Reasonable as Bostock's welfare criteria are, humans incarcerated in prisons may comply with all of
them, exhibiting longevity, medical treatment, lack of signs of abnormal
behavior, and preservation of reproductive capacity. Yet these signs emphatically do not prove that a life in a prison is not a severe compromise
of one's welfare. Even if zoos could be shown to *improve*, rather than
merely maintain, the animal's welfare, this boon would not manage to

---

[1] *Zoos and Animal Rights: The Ethics of Keeping Animals* (London: Routledge, 1993).
Relevant, too, are some of the papers in B. G. Norton et al., eds., *Ethics on the Ark: Zoos,
Animal Welfare, and Wildlife Conservation* (Washington, DC: Smithsonian Institution
Press, 1996).

dissipate a sense of moral dubiousness brought out when one mulls over the viability of utilizing this excuse for other right-possessing beings. The high child mortality rates in some parts of the world justify no one in transporting these children to captivity compensated by longevity and medical treatment.

Bostock is obliged to back up his contention that furthering interests morally validates the trumping of freedom. He does this in a surprising manner: undermining the assumption that captivity is a form of cruelty. He argues for this conclusion by distinguishing between various forms of cruelty, refusing to regard captivity as constituting any of them. This (intriguing) result is achieved through limiting the relevant forms of cruelty either to unjustifiably causing suffering or to taking pleasure in doing so (56). For Bostock, captivity does not fall under gratuitous or sadistic creation of pain, ergo, it does not constitute cruelty.

Yet why restrict the scope of cruelty in this way? How about actions such as a systematic thwarting of an entity's potential, or a frustration of its broader instincts? In human contexts we readily acknowledge that cruelty need not necessarily relate to the creation of pain. Some eventualities are envisioned as a horrifying prospect while, if occurring, they might not be experienced as painful at all. Consider coma. Creating such a state in another is surely cruel. A gruesome example would be inducing a human baby into permanent coma. Setting aside the suffering of those related to the baby or those hearing of the horrifying deed (for the sake of the argument, assume that the baby is unrelated to anyone, and that no one will learn of its fate), such could constitute an innocuous act according to Bostock's stipulations, merely because it does not generate suffering.

AGAINST THE WELFARE DEFENSE OF ZOOS

Analogies such as these are precarious. Notwithstanding the overlap between abusing humans and maltreating animals, the important dissimilarities between humans and nonhumans call for a species-sensitive understanding of cruelty. Can Bostock plausibly dismiss the above counter example to his claim, based on an alleged disanalogy between humans and nonhumans?

Although we need to develop a refined species-sensitive understanding of cruelty, I cannot envision a defensible rendering of it that would help Bostock. His understanding of cruelty is much too narrow. Unjustifiably inducing coma in a young giraffe or a buffalo is an instance of (painless) cruelty because it is a severe form of deprivation. Like the human baby, the lack of awareness or experience of this deprivation does not purge the act. The severe limiting of movement that zoos rely on is arguably a *worse* form of deprivation because, for many animals, it is experienced as such (behavioral problems and the disinclination to breed in captivity suggest this). To begin with, Bostock would accordingly have to broaden his definition of cruelty so that it would include deprivation. Fine-tuning "deprivation" so that it would be a species-sensitive moral operator is surely important. Yet for our purposes we may leave it vague: deprivation would minimally include action such as severe restriction of movement. This stipulation alone would rule out many of the animal exhibits that we see in our zoos. For, while a species-sensitive unpacking of "severe restriction of movement" would not entail that nonhuman animals require unlimited freedom of movement (human beings do not possess unlimited freedom of movement either), animals such as primates, the larger predators, birds, and many others are "severely" restricted in movement in our zoos. They are being unnecessarily deprived. We are being cruel.

Can Bostock modify his claims so that his defense of zoos would pertain only to those animals that are *mildly* deprived by their captivity? He cannot. This is due to a difference between farm/companion animals on the one hand, and zoo animals on the other, a difference that underlies a broader and more comprehensive rejection of zoos (a rejection that, incidentally, makes it unnecessary to introduce a finer distinction between severe and mild restriction of movement). The relevant difference relates to paternalism and to the very act of placing animals in captivity. As suggested earlier, permanent paternalistic relations among healthy human beings are by definition immoral. In the case of (some) nonhuman animals, paternalism is accepted as justified by most liberationists. This difference accounts for our predilection to regard imprisoning humans for their own good as sophistry, and at the same time allowing this very same argument to carry considerable weight when it comes to limiting movement of nonhuman animals. The moral justification for such favoritism regarding paternalism appeals to the overall good of these animals: farm animals and numerous companion animals owe their existence to the decision of human beings to place them in such permanent paternalistic relations, and this can be done without abusing or exploiting them. Yet unlike cows, pigs, hens, or sheep, zoo animals such as tigers, elephants, snakes, penguins, zebras, parrots, and other crowd pullers all live outside human supervision and do so successfully. They might, as Bostock says, live longer in a zoo, and lead an overall healthier life. But unlike farm animals, the *existence* of such animals does not depend on human action. If we avoid hunting them down or destroying their ecosystems they can survive. Placing them inside cages is accordingly *not* in their interests. In the rare cases in which it is (e.g., wounded animals or an endangered species), captivity can be considered a good only if it is conceived as a temporary stage, preparatory for the eventual release of the animal.

To conclude: a welfare-based paternalism with regard to zoo animals is ill-founded. Bostock's defense of zoos—which is predicated on such paternalism—is to be rejected.

Two Objections

Here are two objections to what I have just said:

1. Paternalism with regards to animals is always wrong, whether it relates to companion animals, farm animals, or zoo animals. Accordingly, my attempt to set a meaningful difference between justified and unjustified paternalism is questionable and self-serving: animals are better off the more freedom they have. I do not need to respond to this objection since, in the context of zoos, this argument involves dismissing the moral legitimacy of zoos and does not oppose my general conclusion.[2]
2. If I am granting that some version of paternalism is credible with regard to farm animals, I cannot bar plausible extensions of such justifications to zoo animals.

In detail, the counterargument in (2) is this: when justifying keeping farm animals, I allowed that being brought into a qualitatively good existence is an overall good for the animal. This, in turn, legitimated practices in which the animal will be used (though not exploited). I claimed that wild animals can easily live outside the interaction with humans, whereas domestic animals will most probably die. Yet this claim is probably false as a categorical claim about species as such (small numbers of domesticated animals may well survive in feral populations, perhaps in specially formed reserves). When considering individual animals (rather than species), it is plausible that the capacity of zoos to keep animals safe and within reach of medical intervention saves many *individual* lives of animals, thus promoting their welfare, and is accordingly justified in their case. A decision to banish zoos will also lead to problems with the animals that are already kept and were born in them. For those numerous individual animals, a decision to release them in the wild would be dangerous or fatal. Abrogating zoos is detrimental to the welfare of these individual animals. In conclusion, if we accept some version of the idea that elevating

---

[2] For the same reason I avoid discussing other objections to zoos (rights-based criticisms or the rejection of zoos on symbolic grounds: zoos epitomizing instrumental control and objectification of animals and nature parading under the banners of entertainment or education).

welfare excuses a restricting of freedom, we have to concede that in many individual cases, keeping wild animals in zoos is a justified practice.

The reply to this is that a negative evaluation of a practice does not stand or fall on individual success stories. Objectionable practices—e.g., prostitution or child labor—can sometimes give rise to examples of individual victims who have surprisingly gained something through such practices, yet this does not modify the moral status of the practice as such. If one grants that zoos are involved in the prima facie wrong of depriving an animal of its freedom, the fact that some individual animals might benefit from zoos is no more of a justification of zoos than implausibly defending the practices above by pointing out exceptional cases. Moreover, banishing zoos cannot mean that the animals who are already in zoos and who cannot be released will be killed. Alternatives to this are not hard to imagine.

Companion and farm animals are also deprived of their freedom. Why does curtailing freedom seem harsher in the case of zoos? The reply relates to alternatives: while too many companion animals are abused, and although most zoos are morally superior to modern factory-farming, domestic animals *can* be brought into a life of interaction with humans that is also morally acceptable. When such animals are kept in spacious quarters, when they lead comfortable, safe, and long lives, when they are not isolated, they can be maintained in paternalistic, give-and-take relations with humans that improve their overall welfare. Billions of such qualitatively good lives will not be lived if these animal-related practices are abolished. Dogs, cats, horses, cows, sheep, and hens all appear to require some space for grazing and/or exercise, but given such space their lives with humans appear to be good ones (caged birds or reptiles kept as domestic animals are on the same moral footing as zoo animals). The same cannot be said for most wild animals held in zoos. A laying hen can be kept by humans in a morally acceptable way. A lion, a bear, a chimpanzee, or an antelope cannot.

Or, at least not in a zoo. The previous argument obviously does not apply to reserves in which humans may watch wild animals from their cars or on foot. How about drive-through theme parks that usually allow wild animals much of what they need and also satisfy the educational objectives of zoos? Or the very rare zoos that manage to create rich natural enclosures that duplicate the natural surroundings for the animals? Size matters. And if a pack of chimps is kept in a fenced park that is large enough, such a life does not involve deprivation.[3]

---

[3] Bostock, *Zoos and Animal Rights*, chap. 7 is very helpful on types of exhibits and what may constitute a "duplication" of natural surroundings for an animal. I permit myself to remain programmatic: the argument advanced here opposed all of the zoos I have visited, including ones that invest much in the welfare of the animals kept in them. But I cannot rule

But the argument against such progressive enclosures is not that they create deprivation (as do the inferior zoos), but that they rely on the wrong form of paternalism. The animals kept in such parks can survive without them being initially captured in the wild and reintroduced into these new surroundings. This last claim is obviously amenable to change: species become endangered and may become extinct without human intervention. If reintroducing such animals into a safer environment becomes mandatory, drive-through parks are the lesser of two evils. Such parks would include only those endangered animals. Allowing visitors to watch them as a form of education or amusement and thus obtaining partial funding for these enterprises is morally permissible, since the paternalism on which these institutions are predicated is of the right kind.

One way through which educational needs can be met without compromising the moral claims of nonhuman animals is through exhibits of embalmed animals. My model here is the wonderful and detailed exhibit maintained by the Chicago-based Field Museum. A liberationist would have to insist that the animals used in such a way were not hunted down first. But given this proviso, such exhibits involve no suffering and enable study of the animals. Cultural analyses of zoos often note how they are institutionally placed between the circus and the museum.[4] Presenting dead rather than living animals surely makes for an entirely different institution and experience than the one offered by zoos. Yet natural history museums can meet the need to know or educate (which zoos claim they are advancing) without the cruelty that zoos create.

To conclude: zoos present a tough case for moderate liberationists. If paternalism with regard to nonhuman animals is sometimes permissible, zoos appear to be worthy examples of such paternalism, since they often present themselves as a new kind of Ark, there to preserve and salvage endangered animals. I argued that such a position is to be rejected: an overwhelming majority of actual zoo exhibits involve deprivation that is experienced as such. A significant portion of them induce deprivation without it being experienced as such, yet it is still morally wrong. Zoos are predicated on the wrong form of paternalism, one that unjustifiably intervenes in the lives of animals that can survive without human assistance. I have given some examples of cases in which temporary captivity of wild animals can be morally vindicated. Yet, on the whole, (even moderate) liberationists should oppose zoos.

---

out the possibility that some other zoo, or a future one, will manage to re-create a habitat for its animals that does not constitute a deprivation.

[4] B. Mullan and G. Marvin, *Zoo Culture* (Urbana: University of Illinois Press, 1987); R. Malamud, Reading Zoos: Representations of Animals and Captivity (New York: New York University Press, 1998).

CONCLUSION

THE TURKEY I HAD SLAUGHTERED was not the last animal I ate. But, aside from rare successes at fishing, it was the only animal that I had personally killed and eaten. I was about twenty at the time, in my military service, and was overseeing a group of soldiers for an off-camp activity. One soldier came up with the idea of purchasing a turkey from a nearby breeder and slaughtering it later. I approved. After selecting a bird from a farm and driving with it back to base, we circled it and proceeded to try to kill it. We used knives.

A turkey is a large animal. One gets a sense of how big it is when one needs to approach and control it. The soldier who initiated the idea had promised that the killing would be a piece of cake, and that he had often done it. He forgot that his experience was with hens, not turkeys. Moreover, the knife he possessed was blunt. This meant that after we finally managed to restrain the turkey, instead of a clean kill the agonized bird was struggling under us with a series of cuts in its neck, trying to get away. It was not dying. At one point, someone suggested that we pin the neck down on the ground, attach the knife to the bird's neck, with the soldier with the blunt knife standing on top of the knife itself. That did it. The animal died, and we proceeded to skin and eat it. Ironically, all this took place as part of advanced training in combat medicine—we were all teachers of combat medicine, trained to alleviate suffering and save lives.

I had virtually forgotten about this event. It did not turn me into a vegetarian or prevent me from enjoying meat during that evening or the years that followed (I became a vegetarian only about fifteen years later). But in conclusion, it is that memory that prompts me to record it, and I allow it, because in writing this book I have been diligently avoiding all emotional appeals, or striving to establish empathy to animals, or trying to horrify my reader into liberationism. So after cleansing this book (perhaps too thoroughly) from anything sentimental ("sentimentality" being a standard charge leveled against the liberationist argument), I can close with this personal anecdote.

I find that relating this grisly confession is appropriate since it captures many of the regrettable attitudes that this book aims to transform. We first have the happy association between eating meat and social pleasure. We then move to the quasi-ritualistic attempt to upgrade a predictable barbeque by slaughtering the animal ourselves, along with the excitement that this promises. Then we have the striking gap, the discovery that the transition from a live entity into food is not smooth, and that it was precisely our incompetence at killing that enabled the animal to powerfully register its resistance and establish this gap.

What we lacked was not an acknowledgment of some basic equality between people and animals. Nor was it our speciesism that was at fault. We were simply the standard stone-hearted products of a society for which the living animal is merely a transition phase on the way to becoming food. The fierce opposition of the animal registered something that slipped through the overarching instrumentalization and objectification that we imposed on it, something that we were unprepared to digest, which is what, perhaps, may have imprinted this memory in me.

Transforming objectification need not depend on a sweeping overthrow of our speciesist worldview. We can, if we wish, retain most of our biases and preferences. We need only attend diligently and consistently to the beliefs that we actually hold in order to perceive where our practice needs to be reformed. This book's deflation of the case for animals aims to show that there is nothing overly complex or morally groundbreaking in the argument on behalf of animals. The ascription of rights to animals and the endorsement of utilitarianism are unnecessary. Liberationism follows from the simplest argument within applied ethics, one that even a child can follow: tremendous suffering and large-scale killing take place. These can be avoided. We need to try to do so. One can argue over (some) of the details, but if the moral logic in this rudimentary piece of reasoning is flawed, then something is fundamentally wrong in our core moral beliefs.

Broad social transformations in some parts of the world—the eradication of slavery, the disappearance of class-based society, the improvement in the status of women, the tolerance for lifestyles that were violently persecuted in the past—inspire the hope that what was once considered a universal and uncontroversial given can be questioned and substantially reformed. Abandoning convenient habits due to moral concerns is never easy. But, should it occur, such can only take place after attaining moral clarity regarding one's obligations. Animal ethics has played an important role in this process in recent decades. We can do more.